How to

Prevent Special Education Litigation

How to

Prevent Special Education Litigation

EIGHT LEGAL LESSON PLANS

Regina Umpstead

Janet R. Decker

Kevin P. Brady

David Schimmel

Matthew Militello

TEACHERS COLLEGE PRESS

TEACHERS COLLEGE | COLUMBIA UNIVERSITY

NEW YORK AND LONDON

Published by Teachers College Press, 1234 Amsterdam Avenue, New York, NY 10027

Table 3.1 is used with permission of the Disability Rights Education and Defense Fund (DREDF).

"Top Ten Methods to Foster IEP Team Collaboration," appearing in Lesson 8, is used with permission of Dave Goldberg.

Library of Congress Cataloging-in-Publication Data

Preventing special education litigation : eight legal lesson plans Regina Umpstead [and four others].
pages cm
Includes bibliographical references and index.
ISBN 978-0-8077-5707-9 (pbk.)—ISBN 978-0-8077-7415-1 (ebook)
1. Special education—Law and legislation—United States. 2. Educational law and legislation—United States. I. Umpstead, Regina, author.
KF4209.3.P74 2015
344.73′0791—dc23

2015014943

ISBN 978-0-8077-5707-9 (paper)
ISBN 978-0-8077-7415-1 (ebook)

Printed on acid-free paper
Manufactured in the United States of America

22 21 20 19 18 17 16 15 8 7 6 5 4 3 2 1

Contents

Acknowledgments **vii**

Introduction and Overview **1**

Why This Book Is Needed 1

The Purpose of This Book 2

How to Use This Book 2

Overview of the Lessons 3

Organization of Each Lesson 4

References 5

Lesson 1
Why Learn About Special Education Law? **7**

Introduction for Facilitators 7

Materials Needed 8

Hook 9

Background, Purpose, and Objectives of the Lesson 9

Activity 11

Questions for Conversation 15

Test Your Knowledge 16

Additional Resources 16

References 17

Lesson 2
What Are the Main Federal Entitlements and Protections? **19**

Introduction for Facilitators 19

Materials Needed 20

Hook 20

Background, Purpose, and Objectives of the Lesson 21

Activity 22

Questions for Conversation 27

Test Your Knowledge 28

Additional Resources 31

References 32

Lesson 3
Who Is Eligible for Special Education? **33**

Introduction for Facilitators 33

Materials Needed 35

Hook 35

Background, Purpose, and Objectives of the Lesson 36

Activity 37

Questions for Conversation 40

Test Your Knowledge 41

Additional Resources 42

References 42

Lesson 4
How Can We Ensure an Appropriate IEP? **43**

Introduction for Facilitators 43

Materials Needed 44

Background, Purpose, and Objectives of the Lesson 44

Hook 45

Activity 47

Questions for Conversation 52

Test Your Knowledge 54

Additional Resources 56

References 56

Lesson 5
What Does It Mean to Teach Students in the Least Restrictive Environment? 58

Introduction for Facilitators 58

Materials Needed 58

Hook 59

Background, Purpose, and Objectives of the Lesson 59

Activity 64

Questions for Conversation 67

Test Your Knowledge 69

Additional Resources 69

References 69

Lesson 6
How Are Students with Disabilities Disciplined Differently? 70

Introduction for Facilitators 70

Materials Needed 71

Hook 71

Background, Purpose and Objectives of the Lesson 73

Activity 74

Questions for Conversation 78

Test Your Knowledge 81

Additional Resources 82

References 83

Lesson 7
Why Must We Plan for Students' Lives Beyond High School? 84

Introduction for Facilitators 84

Materials Needed 85

Hook 85

Background, Purpose, and Objectives of the Lesson 87

Activity 87

Questions for Conversation 88

Test Your Knowledge 90

Additional Resources 93

References 93

Lesson 8
Why Is Fostering Positive Family-School Relationships Important? 94

Introduction for Facilitators 94

Materials Needed 94

Hook 95

Background, Purpose and Objectives of the Lesson 96

Activity 96

Questions for Conversation 97

Test Your Knowledge 99

Additional Resources 100

References 100

Appendix
What Is the Basic Legal Framework Related to Students with Disabilities? 101

References 105

Index 107

About the Authors 115

Acknowledgments

We begin by acknowledging that this book would not have been possible if it were not for the previous work of David Schimmel, Suzanne Eckes, and Matthew Militello that appears in their book, *Principals Teaching the Law: 10 Legal Lessons Your Teachers Must Know* (Corwin Press, 2010). Thank you for your inspiration.

Next, we thank the individuals who took the time to provide us with detailed feedback as we prepared this book. We appreciate your generosity in sharing your expertise in special education law matters and your dedication to supporting the education of students with disabilities: Adam Blanchard, Chippewa Valley Schools (Michigan); Susan Bon, University of South Carolina; Cassandra Cole, Indiana University; Heather Cole, The University of Texas; Jean B. Crockett, University of Florida; Daniel Harbottle, Harbottle Law Group (California); Constance Lyttle, Drexel University (Pennsylvania); Patrick Mahon, High Tech High (California); Martha McCarthy, Loyola Marymount University (California); Michel Miller O'Neal, Drexel University (Pennsylvania); Allan Osborne (Retired), Sung Harbor Community School (Massachusetts); Barbara Pazey, The University of Texas at Austin; Charlie Russo, University of Dayton (Ohio); Edward Sabornie, North Carolina State University; Elizabeth Shaver, University of Akron School of Law (Ohio); Jeanne Surface, University of Nebraska; Mark C. Weber, DePaul University School of Law (Illinois); and Mitchell Yell, University of South Carolina.

We would like to extend a special thank-you to Linda Weiss, who spent countless hours editing and organizing this work prior to its publication. Thank you for your support and dedication.

Finally, we thank the educators across the United States who daily devote their lives to educating our nation's youth.

—Regina Umpstead
Janet R. Decker
Kevin P. Brady
David Schimmel
Matthew Militello

Introduction and Overview

As faculty members in education law and policy from five different universities around the country, we wrote this book because we discovered that it is needed. All educators and school leaders must be informed about the legal rights of students with disabilities; however, research documents—and we have observed in our classrooms—that many educators are woefully underprepared in special education law. This introductory chapter explains why educators should become better informed about legal issues related to students with disabilities. It also provides an overview of the book's purpose, content, and organization.

WHY THIS BOOK IS NEEDED

A national survey found that the vast majority of American teachers have taken no courses in school law in either their preservice or inservice programs (Schimmel & Militello, 2007). The survey also revealed that as a result, most teachers are uninformed or misinformed about their basic legal rights and responsibilities and those of their students. This lack of information is especially evident regarding special education laws that impact almost every public school and even nonpublic schools.

The fact that teachers are poorly informed about special education law is a serious problem for three reasons. First, there is more litigation involving special education issues than any other area of school law (Katsiyannis & Herbst, 2004). In fact, legal scholars have warned that special education is one of the "most contentious" and "important" topics in school law (Eckes, 2008, pp. 8–9). Second, because many educators are confused about special education law, they unintentionally violate their students' rights and fail to carry out their legal responsibilities (Schimmel, Eckes, & Militello, 2010). Even though over half of students with disabilities are now educated in general education classrooms (Institute of Education Sciences, 2010), most teachers are not required to complete coursework in special education (Institute of Education Sciences, 2010). As a result, educators may unwittingly expose themselves and their respective schools to liability for violating the rights of students with disabilities (Katsiyannis, Losinski, & Prince, 2012). Third, when educators describe what legal issues most concern them, special education is often at the top of the list. According to one school superintendent, "Special education is perhaps the most complex and emotional aspect of public school life" (Berlin, 2009, p. 734).

For these three reasons, there is a critical need to help school personnel become legally literate about special education. Both special education directors and school principals are in a unique position to meet this need and to provide their colleagues with necessary information about special education laws. Many school leaders, however, do not feel they have the time, content knowledge, or teaching materials that are essential to help their staff learn about special education mandates (Militello, Schimmel, & Eberwein, 2009).

THE PURPOSE OF THIS BOOK

We have written this book in order to meet the critical need for special education law instruction in schools. The book is not intended to replace the important consultation that occurs between school employees and their attorneys. Therefore, nothing in this book should be construed as legal advice and should not be acted on as such. Instead, our book presents legal information intended to provide educators with the legal knowledge, understanding, and skills that enable them to apply relevant legal rules to their everyday practice. Its goal is not to help educators win in court; instead, its purpose is to help educators stay out of court by practicing preventive law. Although other scholarly books exist about special education law, this is the *only* book designed to provide busy school leaders with the materials they need to inform and educate teachers and other school officials about the basic principles of special education law.

When school leaders become effective law teachers, their staff members will be able to obtain information they need about special education law from a reliable source, rather than from the rumors and myths swirling around the teachers' lounge. By having legally literate staff who can spot and prevent legal issues from occurring, school districts will benefit because their educators will make fewer legal mistakes. Consequently, educators' adherence to legal requirements of special education should reduce the time and energy that busy school leaders must devote to dealing with violations of the law and subsequent litigation, fielding and resolving parental complaints about special education, and correcting inadvertent errors by school employees. Equipped with a clear understanding of the basic requirements of special education law, educators will be able to uphold the law with confidence, and will be empowered to protect their students' educational rights, their schools' exposure to liability, and their own educational practices.

HOW TO USE THIS BOOK

The authors have designed the special education legal lessons in this book especially for busy professionals with no prior legal training. The book includes eight easy-to-implement legal lessons within a prepackaged curriculum; therefore, no lengthy preparation is necessary. We have written the lessons in a straightforward manner using easy-to-understand terminology, not legal jargon. Any educator can teach the lessons; therefore, special education directors, principals, assistant principals, teachers, and other school professionals can teach their colleagues about special education law. In addition, university instructors can incorporate the book into their courses as they educate future teachers and administrators about special education.

This book contains all the necessary materials and scripts, so that the facilitators of the lessons simply need to deliver the content provided. The lessons are interactive in order to maintain the active engagement of the participants. After each lesson, facilitators may use measurable objectives and assessments to ensure that the participants learned the intended content of the lesson.

Because each lesson takes approximately 1 hour to complete, educators can use this book in a variety of ways. School officials can include the lessons as part of faculty meetings or other professional development sessions. For example, a special education director or principal might lead a group of teachers through a lesson, conduct the postlesson assessment, and review the results with teachers. Alternatively, a principal may wish to assign different groups of teachers to lead lessons at each faculty meeting throughout the year. Educators can also tailor the lessons to suit the needs of an individual school or district. Finally, university professors may wish to assign a lesson as an individual or group assignment for students to review, then present to their classmates.

OVERVIEW OF THE LESSONS

This book addresses important special education legal issues occurring in schools today. All of the lessons utilize actual situations that have led to expensive litigation. Topics include:

- Individuals with Disabilities Education Act (IDEA)
- Section 504 of the Rehabilitation Act of 1973 (Section 504)
- Americans with Disabilities Act (ADA)
- Eligibility
- Response to Intervention (RtI)
- Free Appropriate Public Education (FAPE)
- Individualized Education Programs (IEPs)
- Least Restrictive Environment (LRE)
- Discipline
- Due Process Hearings and Alternative Dispute Resolution
- Transition Services
- Parental Participation and Advocacy.

The content appears in the following eight lesson plans:

Lesson 1: Why Learn About Special Education Law?
Lesson 2: What Are the Main Federal Entitlements and Protections?
Lesson 3: Who Is Eligible for Special Education?
Lesson 4: How Can We Ensure an Appropriate IEP?
Lesson 5: What Does It Mean to Teach Students in the Least Restrictive Environment?
Lesson 6: How Are Students with Disabilities Disciplined Differently?
Lesson 7: Why Must We Plan for Students' Lives Lives Beyond High School?
Lesson 8: Why Is Fostering Family-School Relationships Important?

ORGANIZATION OF EACH LESSON

Each lesson begins with an Introduction for Facilitators designed to provide the facilitators with a brief background on why the topic is significant. The remainder of each lesson includes the following sections:

- Introduction for Facilitators
- Materials Needed
- Hook
- Background, Purpose, and Objectives
- Activities
- Questions for Conversation
- Test Your Knowledge
- Additional Resources
- References

The facilitators may present the entire lesson within an hour-long faculty meeting. Alternatively, because every lesson includes predictable time expectations for each subsection, it is also possible to present only a portion of a lesson to teach educators about the law.

Introduction for Facilitators. Facilitators review the Introduction prior to leading the lesson. By doing so, they are aware of the main topics and significance of the lesson.

Materials Needed. Facilitators should also review this section prior to presenting each lesson in order to identify what materials will be needed throughout the lesson (e.g., projector and screen, video clips, dry-erase boards and markers).

Hook. The purpose of the hook—also known as the anticipatory set—is to capture the participants' attention; it should motivate them to want to learn more. Hooks use a variety of strategies such as skits where participants/facilitators role-play common legal dilemmas, and video clips of legal issues followed by participants' discussion.

Background, Purpose, and Objectives. The next section provides the background on the topic, so that the participants have the requisite legal information to complete the lesson's activities. The facilitators also explicitly tell participants the learning objectives for the lesson.

Activities. The participants then have an opportunity to apply the law through engaging in a variety of activities. This interactive format allows them to develop the skills they will need when encountering special education dilemmas in the future. Not only are the participants more likely to remain attentive while engaging in activities, but they will also be more likely to retain their new knowledge than if they were just passively listening to a lecture. Multiple strategies are employed, including asking small groups to analyze different legal cases, reviewing scenarios to spot and analyze legal issues, role-playing responses to a given scenario, and facilitating small-group presentations.

Questions for Conversation. Presenting content is only half the battle. This section contains a set of frequently asked questions and answers. Facilitators can arrange in advance for participants to ask these questions during the presentation, or they can wait for the questions to arise naturally.

Test Your Knowledge. At the end of each lesson, the facilitators will assess participants' knowledge of the topic. Facilitators will not always include a formal assessment, but may instead use some other strategy to ascertain the participants' knowledge. Examples of assessments include written quizzes and activities where participants view skits and are to spot legal violations portrayed in it.

Additional Resources. Facilitators can choose to learn more about each lesson's content by consulting additional materials that are listed in the book. The resources include relevant websites, books, and articles that can be referenced for further information.

References. The last section of each lesson plan includes a description of any resources used to create the lesson. Citations to relevant laws, cases, and secondary sources are listed.

REFERENCES

Berlin, L. F. (2009). Public school law: What does it mean in the trenches? *Phi Delta Kappan, 90*(10), 733–736.

Eckes, S. E. (2008). Significant legal issues for inclusion in pre-service teacher preparation. *Action in Teacher Education, 30*(2), 25–35.

Institute of Education Sciences. (2010, July). Do states have certification requirements for preparing general education teachers to teach students with disabilities? Experience in the Northeast and Islands Region. Institute for Educational Sciences, No. 090. Retrieved from http://ies.ed.gov/ncee/edlabs/projects/project.asp?ProjectID=238

Katsiyannis, A., & Herbst, M. (2004). 20 ways to minimize litigation in special education. *Intervention in School and Clinic, 40,* 106–110.

Katsiyannis, A., Losinski, M., & Prince, A. (2012). Litigation and students with disabilities: A persistent concern. *NASSP Bulletin, 96*(1), 23–43.

Militello, M., Schimmel, D., & Eberwein, H. J. (2009). If they knew, they would change: How legal knowledge impacts principals' practice. *NASSP Bulletin, 93*(1), 27–52.

Schimmel, D., Eckes, S., & Militello, M. (2010). *Principals teaching the law: 10 legal lessons your teachers must know.* Thousand Oaks, CA: Corwin Press.

Schimmel, D., & Militello, M. (2007). Legal literacy for teachers: A neglected responsibility. *Harvard Educational Review, 77*(3), 257–284.

Why Learn About Special Education Law?

INTRODUCTION FOR FACILITATORS

Special education law is vital for all educators to understand, yet many educators remain uninformed and unaware of both the rights of students with disabilities and the policies designed to protect those rights. This lack of educator training has led to unequal treatment, discrimination, and even abuse of students with disabilities in schools.

In a 2009 report, the U.S. Government Accountability Office (GAO) reported misuse of restraints and seclusion by school personnel, sometimes causing serious injury or death of students with disabilities (U.S. GAO, 2009). In 2014, the U.S. Department of Education Office for Civil Rights (OCR) issued a report that found that although students with disabilities represent only 12% of the student population, nearly 60% of students placed in seclusion and 75% of those physically restrained at school are students with disabilities (U.S. Department of Education OCR, 2014). Additionally, OCR reported that suspension rates for students with disabilities are twice as high (13%) as for students without disabilities (6%; U.S. Department of Education OCR, 2014). The most common type of lawsuit filed against schools involves allegations that school districts have violated the legal entitlements and protections of students with disabilities (Katsiyannis & Herbst, 2004).

Despite over 40 years of increased legal protections for students with disabilities, problems persist because school administrators and educators have been woefully underprepared to apply the principles of special education law to their daily practices. Ignorance of special education law does not excuse a school district from being held legally responsible, yet the vast majority of states do not require principals to complete any formal coursework in special education law. Similarly, although most states require teachers to gain *experience* working with students with disabilities before receiving their teacher certification, only about one-half of those states require formal *coursework* to be completed in special education (Institute of Education Sciences, 2010).

Administrators and educators want more training in legal issues surrounding special education (Davidson & Algozzine, 2002). Because special education law is comprised of a variety of federal and state statutes, regulations, and court decisions, it may seem like a complicated maze that is difficult to navigate. However, many key features of special education law are relatively simple to understand; yet uninformed educators are prone to unintentionally violate even these "simple" rules in practice. For instance, every teacher of a student with disabilities has a basic duty to review and comply with the student's Individualized Education Program (IEP), a document that describes the special education and related services a student with disabilities is legally entitled to receive; numerous teachers, however, report never receiving and/or reading their students' IEPs, much less complying with their terms.

To remedy the shortfall in the preservice training of teachers and administrators, school districts must provide targeted professional development on special education law (Pazey & Cole, 2013). Although it may be difficult for busy administrators to devote time to this needed legal training, that same training may prevent unnecessary anxiety, unwitting violations of law, and expensive litigation. Most importantly, it should also lead to better outcomes for students with disabilities.

The lesson plans contained in this book will outline specialized training for school employees to avoid litigation and to improve the education of students with disabilities. This first lesson sets the stage for the remaining seven lessons in this book by introducing special education law and providing participants with a rationale and incentive to learn more. The historical context underlying special education law serves as a backdrop to help participants understand why past discrimination and systematic exclusion compelled Congress to enact laws such as the Individuals with Disabilities Education Act (IDEA, 2006), Americans with Disabilities Act (ADA, 1990, 2008), and Section 504 of the Rehabilitation Act of 1973 (Section 504).

It is likely that participants will ask a number of questions during this legal lesson that relate to the other lessons in this book. If this occurs, facilitators should avoid allowing the conversation to meander off-topic and explain that this lesson is only the first of many legal lessons on special education law. The estimated time needed for each portion of the lesson follows each heading and the entire lesson should take approximately 1 hour to facilitate.

MATERIALS NEEDED

The facilitator(s) should organize the following items prior to the lesson:

- LCD projector, screen, and Internet connection to show video (see *Hook*);
- Facilitator script (see Background, Purpose, and Objectives);
- Game directions, Historical Event cards, Current Event cards, and coins (see *Activity*);
- Questions typed or written on three handouts (see *Questions for Conversation*);
- Index cards for each participant (see *Test Your Knowledge*); and
- Optional: Objectives visually displayed (see *Background, Purpose, and Objectives*).

HOOK (5 MINUTES)

1. To begin the lesson, the facilitator will ask participants to view the video linked here, entitled "Lives Worth Living": http://www.youtube.com/watch?v=RlXm9NJDacM&feature=player_embedded (Neudel, 2011). This video is a 2½-minute PBS documentary segment illustrating the historical segregation of individuals with disabilities and the advocacy efforts that led to the educational inclusion of students with disabilities.
2. Immediately following the video, the facilitator will lead a large-group discussion that is described in the next section.

BACKGROUND, PURPOSE, AND OBJECTIVES OF THE LESSON (20 MINUTES)

Next, the facilitators will read the following **Facilitator Script** to the participants or paraphrase the information in their own words (if there is more than one facilitator, you may choose to split the script among them). The facilitators should consider displaying the objectives visually so that the participants can reference them during the lesson.

Facilitator Script

Facilitator: The video you just watched discussed legislation including the Americans with Disabilities Act or "ADA." The ADA is a federal law that extended the reach of Section 504 of the Rehabilitation Act of 1973, which is commonly referred to as "Section 504." In addition to the ADA and Section 504, Congress enacted the Individuals with Disabilities Education Act, or "IDEA," in 1975. We will discuss these three laws in much more detail in future lessons. Before these three disability laws existed, many individuals with disabilities faced dismal living and learning environments. Some were segregated in highly restrictive settings such as state institutions that were built to protect society from the perceived negative influences of individuals diagnosed with mental illness (Pazey & Yates, 2012). Many of these institutions only provided shelter, with minimal food and clothing. Before the laws were enacted, more attention was placed on providing basic care to students with disabilities rather than providing education and rehabilitation (U.S. Department of Education, 2010). Turn to a neighbor and discuss whether you believe discrimination against individuals with disabilities still exists today, even though laws such as the ADA, Section 504, and the IDEA are in force.

Facilitator: *[Allow participants to discuss what you just told them for a few minutes, then ask]* What do you think? Does discrimination against individuals with disabilities still exist today?

Facilitator: *[Field responses from the participants, then explain]* We may only have limited influence on what occurs in society, but as a school district, we can influence the educational opportunities that we provide to our students, including those with disabilities. Therefore, we will be providing a series of professional development sessions devoted to special education law. By a show of hands, how many of you have received training in special education law? What did your training entail?

Facilitator: *[Field responses from the participants, then explain]* Research has found that special education disputes frequently occur because educators and administrators often lack effective training in special education law. As a result, teachers and administrators may not be aware of their legal obligations and, thus, may unintentionally violate the law. This may explain why special education lawsuits are the most common source of education litigation (Katsiyannis & Herbst, 2004). The purpose of providing this training is to educate you about special education law so you will be better able to understand the legal entitlements of students with disabilities and avoid litigation. But you may be wondering why you, personally, need to learn more about special education law, so let's discuss how many students with disabilities you teach. What percentage of students in the general population do you believe are students who receive special education and related services?

Facilitator: *[Field responses from the participants, then clarify]* Approximately 13% of students receive special education and related services (U.S. Department of Education, National Center for Education Statistics, 2013), and every student who has been diagnosed with a disability has certain legal entitlements. From 2000–2010, the total number of students eligible under the IDEA increased by more than 150,000, to over 6.4 million children being served by the IDEA in 2010 (National Center for Education Statistics, 2013). In light of these growing numbers, what percentage of students receiving special education services do you think spend all or part of the school day in general education classrooms? By a show of hands, do you believe the number of students eligible for special education who are in general education classrooms for part or all of the school day is in the range of 0 to 20%? 20% to 40%? 40% to 60%? More than 60%?

Facilitator: *[Field responses from the participants, then clarify]* A little more than half—or 57%—of students receiving special education services spend 80 percent or more of their school day in general education classrooms (U.S. Department of Education, 2010). Even though teachers are usually designated as either "special education" or "general education," every teacher must be aware of special education issues because every teacher teaches students with disabilities or other unique learning needs. To increase your understanding of special education law, we will be providing a series of professional development sessions on this topic. Today's training will likely cause you to have many additional questions. Please know that today's session will only be an introduction. Additional sessions will go into more depth on a number of topics and answer questions such as:

- What are the main federal entitlements and protections?
- Who is eligible for special education?

- How can we ensure an appropriate IEP?
- What does it mean to teach students in the Least Restrictive Environment?"
- How are students with disabilities disciplined differently?
- Why must we plan for students beyond high school?
- Why is fostering positive family-school relationships important?

The specific objectives for today's lesson are for you to:

- Increase your awareness of the historical and current contexts of special education law, including the exclusion of students with disabilities in public education and the subsequent litigation and legislation.
- Recognize the practical significance of increasing knowledge about special education law.

Please feel free to ask any questions throughout the lesson.

ACTIVITY (30 MINUTES)

Prior to the lesson, the facilitator will prepare game materials based on the number of participants. The facilitator will photocopy the cards below (i.e., Game Directions, Current Event cards, and Historical Background cards).

Then the facilitators will divide the participants into small groups to complete the following board game. Each group will be given a coin, a Game Directions card, a stack of Current Event cards, and a stack of Historical Background cards.

Game Directions

- Place Current Event cards in one stack and Historical Background cards in another stack.
- Players will take turns based on years of experience as a school employee. The player who has been employed by a school the longest will go first.
- To begin play, the first player will flip a coin. If it lands on heads, the player will read the first Current Event card aloud. After reading the Current Event card, all players will answer the question posed by the card. If it lands on tails, the player will read the first Historical Background card aloud. After reading the Historical Background card, all players will collaborate to place the Historical Event card on the table to create a timeline to place the historical events in chronological order.
- If no cards remain in the pile, the players take turns reading the remaining cards in the other pile aloud.
- The game is over when no Current Event or Historical Background cards remain. At this time, players will ask the facilitators to check their timeline for accuracy. *However, it is unlikely that you will finish the game in the time allotted, so there is no need to rush.*

Historical Event: In 1972, a federal court approved a settlement agreement in *Pennsylvania Association for Retarded Citizens (PARC) v. Pennsylvania* that public schools could not deny services to students with intellectual disabilities. Later the same year, another federal court determined in *Mills v. Board of Education* that schools could not expel or refuse to educate students with disabilities by claiming that the schools did not have adequate resources. As a result, students with disabilities have an equal right to be educated and are entitled to full due process protections. These two court cases signaled that public schools could no longer discriminate against students on the basis of disability. Similar to *Brown v. Board of Education* paving the road for greater integration of students on the basis of race, the decisions in *PARC* and *Mills* served as an impetus for increased integration of students with disabilities.

Historical Event: The *PARC* and *Mills* decisions resulted in an onslaught of litigation and changes in state legislation. To ensure consistency in enforcing the right to a Free Appropriate Public Education (FAPE) for students with disabilities across the country, Congress enacted Public Law (P.L.) 94-142 in 1975, which was also known as the Education for All Handicapped Children Act, which became IDEA.

Historical Event: In the 1982 landmark case of *Board of Education v. Rowley,* the U.S. Supreme Court clarified what schools must do to provide a free appropriate public education—or FAPE—as required by P.L. 94-142. Specifically, a school must provide instruction that is designed to meet the unique needs of the student. The Court explained that students with disabilities do not have a right to the best possible education or an education that allows them to achieve their maximum potential. Instead, students are entitled to an education that is "reasonably calculated" to "confer some educational benefit." The Court created the following two-part test to determine whether schools met their FAPE obligations: (1) Has the school followed procedures under P.L. 94-142, and (2) was the IEP developed "to enable the child to receive educational benefits"?

Historical Event: In 1990, Congress reauthorized P.L. 94-142 and renamed it the Individuals with Disabilities Education Act (IDEA). Prior to IDEA, P.L. 94-142 had not been permanent legislation, and would have expired if Congress hadn't reauthorized it. When IDEA was reauthorized in 1990, it required all eligible students with disabilities between the ages of birth and 21 years to be provided with a free appropriate public education, or FAPE, in the least restrictive environment, or LRE. IDEA mandated that educators must also confer with parents/guardians of students with disabilities to develop an Individualized Education Program, or IEP, that outlines special education and related services. IDEA also included elaborate due process protections to ensure that its provisions were enforced.

Historical Event: Congress reauthorized IDEA and changed its name to the "IDEA Amendments of 1997." The Amendments added provisions regarding the discipline of students with disabilities.

Historical Event: In 2004, Congress reauthorized the IDEA Amendments of 1997, and renamed the law the "Individuals with Disabilities Education Improvement Act." Many changes occurred in 2004, including a modification of the 1997 provisions about discipline and evaluating students with learning disabilities. IDEA incorporated the No Child Left Behind Act's (2002) definition of "highly qualified teachers" and specified what is needed for special education teachers to meet that standard. In addition, the 2004 revisions eliminated short-term objectives in IEPs, and Congress directed the states to develop policies to prevent the over-identification of students of color as needing special education.

Current Event: Segregation of students with disabilities continues to exist. In 2014, the New Jersey Department of Education settled a federal lawsuit by agreeing to address statewide segregation (National School Boards Association, 2014a). New Jersey has the highest level of segregated special education settings in the country. Another lawsuit alleging segregation was filed in 2014. A family sued a Tennessee school district, alleging that the district segregated students with intellectual disabilities (ID) away from regular education classrooms. Specifically, the family claimed that only 5% of the district's students with ID were included in regular classrooms. Comparatively, the national average for inclusion of ID students is 17%. Further, only 12% of the district's students with disabilities spent more than two-fifths of the day in regular classrooms, which was much lower than the national rate of 44% (National School Boards Association, 2014b). *Does anyone have experience with other modern-day examples of segregation of students with disabilities? How do you think this issue may be resolved?*

Current Event: A disproportionate number of students of color are identified as needing special education. In 2013, the OCR entered into a voluntary agreement with the Iowa City Community School District after identifying a disproportionate number of African American students as special education students (National School Boards Association, 2013). Specifically, in 2009–2010, African American students comprised 16% of the district's enrollment; however, African American students made up 35% of the students referred for special education evaluation. *Does anyone have experience with other modern-day examples of overrepresentation of students of color being identified as students with disabilities? How do you believe this issue of the overidentification of students of color may be resolved?*

Current Event: More students with disabilities are filing lawsuits under Section 504 than they did in the past. Many people may not consider students such as those who have medical conditions or allergies as disabled. Yet these students' conditions may fit within Section 504's definition of disability, and therefore the students may be eligible for Section 504's protection against discrimination. Even though more cases are being filed under Section 504, students are not necessarily prevailing in these cases. In 2013, a Pennsylvania district court determined that a school district had not violated Section 504 when it required a kindergarten student with a tree-nut allergy to eat lunch alone at a desk in the cafeteria (*T.F. v. Fox Chapel Area Sch. Dist.*, 2013). In 2014, the

Current Event, continued Seventh Circuit Court of Appeals held that a school did not violate Section 504 after school employees deviated from the Section 504 Plan for a student with diabetes (*CTL v. Ashland Sch. Dist.*, 2014). At one point, a school nurse confiscated a student's edible glucose despite a doctor's order to allow the student to self-treat. *Does anyone have experience with other modern-day examples when Section 504 has been used by students with disabilities? What questions do you have about how Section 504 applies?*

Current Event: The discipline of students with disabilities continues to capture national attention. A 2009 report published by the GAO informed Congress about the use and abuse of restraints and seclusion in schools. In this report, the GAO outlined cases of misuse involving restraints and seclusion by school personnel, which sometimes resulted in serious injury or death. The report highlighted the fact that no federal law existed governing the use of such disciplinary methods. State laws regarding restraints and seclusion at schools "vari[ed] widely" at that time (U.S. GAO, 2009). To rectify this, the Senate reintroduced the Keeping All Students Safe Act (KASSA) in February 2014. KASSA focuses on the use of restraints and seclusion with students in public schools. Although KASSA has not been enacted yet, individual states have investigated the use of seclusion and restraint. For example, the Connecticut Department of Education issued a report in 2014 that found that over 33,000 incidents of student restraint or seclusion occurred in the 2012–13 academic year (National School Boards Association, 2014c). *Does anyone have experience with other modern-day examples of issues surrounding the discipline of students with disabilities? How do you believe these issues regarding seclusion and restraint of students with disabilities may be resolved?*

Current Event: Students with disabilities are subject to bullying in schools. After enduring relentless bullying since 9th grade, an 11th-grader named Tyler Long committed suicide. Tyler's parents sued the school district, claiming that the district knew about the bullying, but failed to intervene and train employees to protect Tyler. They maintained that bullying was a major reason why he hanged himself. At school, other students called Tyler "retard," "slow," "faggot," and "stupid." They spit in his food, knocked his books out of his hands, and physically attacked him multiple times. Because Tyler had a disability, his parents sued under Section 504, claiming that their son was unable to receive a Free Appropriate Public Education, or FAPE, due to severe and pervasive harassment. The Eleventh Circuit Court of Appeals found that the school should have done more to address the disability-based harassment. However, the parents did not prevail in their lawsuit because the school's inaction did not rise to the high bar of "deliberate indifference," a legal standard where districts can be held liable for harassment if they fail to take reasonable actions to stop the harassment from enduring. The court concluded that the school had promptly responded to the reported incidents of harassment and that a jury would be unlikely to find that the school's action was clearly unreasonable (*Long v. Murray County Sch. Dist.*, 2013). Does anyone have experience with other modern-day examples of bullying involving students with disabilities? How do you believe the issues surrounding the bullying of students with disabilities may be resolved?

QUESTIONS FOR CONVERSATION (5–10 MINUTES)

Before the lesson, the facilitator will hand out the following questions to three different participants and request that the participants ask the questions during the lesson. The facilitator may ask the selected participants to ask the questions that appear italicized during the lesson or devote time after the Activity portion of the lesson for Q-and-A.

1. How is the IDEA an underfunded mandate? When the IDEA was enacted, Congress stipulated that the federal government would pay 40% of the average per pupil expenditure for each student with a disability; however, Congress has never appropriated that amount (National School Boards Association, Office of Advocacy, 2014). From 1975 until the late 1990s, the federal IDEA funding covered less than 10 percent of the states' special education expenses (Yell, 2016). In the 2004 Reauthorization of the IDEA, Congress made plans to increase funding each year to eventually achieve the original promise of 40% of the states' costs to provide special education services. Yet the IDEA still remains an underfunded mandate. State educational agencies must ensure that local school districts follow the IDEA's mandates even though the federal government has never provided funding to cover 40% of the special education expenses.

2. Discrimination against students with disabilities is something that occurred in the past, but we now have laws prohibiting this type of discrimination that also gives students with disabilities special rights. Has there been a shift where students with disabilities receive more entitlements and protections than they need? Most special education legal scholars would likely answer "no." Although strides have been made to provide students with disabilities legal protections and entitlements, discrimination persists in many areas. For example, students with disabilities are bullied and harassed more than their nondisabled peers (Blake, Lund, Zhou, & Benz, 2012). Furthermore, there is an overrepresentation of students of color receiving special education (Garda, 2005). Many educators and parents are also dissatisfied with the inequities of the due process system that is intended to resolve disputes between school districts and parents or guardians of students with disabilities (Cope-Kasten, 2013). Legal protections and entitlements exist, but difficulties remain in how the law is implemented.

3. Why do all school employees need to learn about special education law when principals and special education directors are in charge of handling special education issues? While administrators handle many of schools' responsibilities regarding special education, teachers and other school employees are on the front lines. They teach and interact with students with disabilities on a regular basis. And as mentioned earlier in this lesson, more than half of the students receiving special education services spend over 80% of the day in general education classrooms. This means that all teachers and support staff are likely to interact with students receiving special education services on a daily basis. If school employees are unaware of the legal protections and entitlements of students with disabilities, they can unintentionally make mistakes that may be difficult to correct. For example, they could fail to provide accommodations or supports that students are legally entitled to receive during classroom activities and assessments. These mistakes may result in lawsuits filed against the school district, and may be used as evidence to support those lawsuits.

Importantly, the purpose behind the IDEA is:

> [T]o ensure that all children with disabilities have access to a free appropriate public education that emphasizes special education and related services designed to meet their unique needs and prepare them for further education, employment, and independent living; to ensure that the rights of children with disabilities and their parents are protected; to help states, localities, educational service agencies, and federal agencies provide for the education of all children with disabilities; and to assess and ensure the effectiveness of efforts to educate children with disabilities (34 C.F.R. § 300.1).

TEST YOUR KNOWLEDGE (5 MINUTES)

The facilitator will give all participants an index card and ask them to write a paragraph about why it is important to learn more about special education law. The facilitator will review the participants' responses and follow up if participants failed to master any of the objectives.

ADDITIONAL RESOURCES

National Dissemination Center for Children with Disabilities. http://nichcy.org/

Russo, C. J., & Osborne, A. G. (2008). *Essential concepts & school-based cases in special education law.* Thousand Oaks, CA: Corwin Press.

U.S. Department of Education (2000). Prohibited disability harassment: Reminder of responsibilities under Section 504 of the Rehabilitation Act of 1973 and Title II of the Americans with Disabilities Act. Retrieved from www.ed.gov/about/offices/list/ocr/docs/disabharassltr.html

U.S. Department of Education (2010). *Dear colleague letter.* Retrieved from http://www2.ed.gov/about/offices/list/ocr/ letters/colleague-201010.html

Weeden, L. D. (2006). An essay: Unfunded federal mandates: The No Child Left Behind Act and the Individuals with Disabilities Education Act. *T. Marshall Law Review, 31,* 239–251.

REFERENCES

Americans with Disabilities Act, 42 U.S.C. §§ 12101 (1990).

Americans with Disabilities Amendments Act, Public Law 110–325, 122 Stat. 3553 (2008).

Blake, J. J., Lund, E. M., Zhou, Q. Z., & Benz, M. R. (2012). National prevalence rates of bully victimization among students with disabilities in the United States. *School Psychology Quarterly, 27,* 210–222.

Board of Educ. of the Hendrick Hudson Central Sch. Dist. v. Rowley, 458 U.S. 176 (1982).

Cope-Kasten, C. (2013). Bidding (fair)well to due process: The need for a fairer final stage in special education dispute resolution. *Journal of Law and Education, 42,* 501–539.

CTL v. Ashland Sch. Dist., 743 F.3d 524 (7th Cir. 2014).

Davidson, D.N., & Algozzine, B. (2002). Administrators' perceptions of special education law. *Journal of Special Education Leadership, 15*(2), 43–48.

DiPaola, M., & Walther-Thomas, C. (2003). Principals and special education: The critical role of school leaders (COPSSE Document No. IB-7E). Gainesville, FL: University of Florida, Center on Personnel Studies in Special Education. Retrieved from http://www.google.com/url?sa=t&rct=j&q =&esrc=s&source=web&cd=3&ved=0CDsQFjAC&url=http%3A%2F%2Fcopsse.education.ufl.edu%2Fcopsse%2Fdocs%2FIB-7E%e2F1p%2FIB-7E.pdf&ei=eAP-UvjDIobSyAHtkICACA&usg= AFQjCNFpQhoVEKPf9HIERsF7sx4WD4wFyw&sig2=WxNMvoEsHjsZRuh7t8yyjA&bvm=bv.61190604,d.aWc.

Garda, R. A. (2005). The new IDEA: Shifting educational paradigms to achieve racial equality in special education. *Alabama Law Review, 56*(4), 1071–1134.

Individuals with Disabilities Education Act, 20 U.S.C. §§ 1400 *et seq.*, 34 C.F.R. §§ 200 *et seq.*(2006).

Institute of Education Sciences. (2010, July). Do states have certification requirements for preparing general education teachers to teach students with disabilities? Experience in the Northeast and Islands Region. Institute for Educational Sciences, No. 090. Retrieved from http://ies.ed.gov/ncee/edlabs/projects/project.asp?ProjectID=238

Katsiyannis, A., & Herbst, M. (2004). 20 ways to minimize litigation in special education. *Intervention in Sch. & Clinic, 40,* 106–110.

Long v. Murray County Sch. Dist., 522 Fed. App'x. 576 (11th Cir. 2013).

Mills v. District of Columbia Bd. of Educ., 348 F. Supp. 869 (D.D.C. 1972).

National Center for Statistics. Digest of education statistics: Children 3 to 21 years old served under Individuals with Disabilities Education Act (IDEA), Part B, by race/ethnicity and age group: 2000–01 through 2011–12. Retrieved from http://nces.ed.gov/programs/digest/ d13/tables/dt13_204.40.asp

National School Boards Association (NSBA). (2013). Iowa district enters into agreement with OCR to address racial disparities in special ed programs. *Legal Clips.* Retrieved from http://legalclips.nsba.org/2013/09/24/iowa-district-enters-into-agreement-with-ocr-to-address-racial-disparities-in-special-ed-programs/

National School Boards Association (NSBA). (2014a). New Jersey settles federal court suit over segregation of special education students. *Legal Clips.* Retrieved from http://legalclips.nsba.org/2014/03/13/new-jersey-settles-federal-court-suit-over-segregation-of-special-education-students/#sthash.WCMxjLqd.dpuf

National School Boards Association (NSBA). (2014b). Suit claims Tennessee district segregates disabled students twice the national average. *Legal Clips.* Retrieved from http://legalclips.nsba.org/2014/03/04/

suit-claims-tennessee-district-segregates-disabled-students-twice-the-national-average/

National School Boards Association (NSBA). (2014c). Connecticut reports autistic students most subjected to seclusion and restraint. *Legal Clips.* Retrieved from http://legalclips.nsba.org/2014/02/13/connecticut-reports-autistic-students-most-subjected-to-seclusion-and-restraint/

National School Board Association (NSBA) Office of Advocacy. (2014, January 14). *Individuals with Disabilities Education Act: Early preparation for reauthorization.* Retrieved from http://www.nsba.org/Advocacy/Key-Issues/SpecialEducation/NSBA-Issue-Brief-Individuals-with-Disabilities-Education-Act-IDEA.pdf

Neudel, E. (Producer & Director). (2011). *Lives worth living* [Film]. Retrieved from http://www.pbs.org/independentlens/lives-worth-living/film.html

No Child Left Behind (NCLB) Act of 2001, Pub. L. No. 107-110, § 115, Stat. 1425 (2002).

Pazey, B. L., & Cole, H. (2013). The role of special education training in the development of socially just leaders: Building an equity consciousness in educational leadership programs. *Educational Administration Quarterly, 49*(2), 243–271. doi:10.1177/0013161X12463934

Pazey, B. L., & Yates, J. R. (2012). Conceptual and historical foundations of special education administration. In J. Crockett, B. Billingsley, & M. L. Boscardin (Eds.), *Handbook of leadership in special education* (pp. 17–36). London: Routledge

Pennsylvania Association for Retarded Children (PARC) v. Pennsylvania, 343 F. Supp. 279 (E.D. PA, 1972).

Schimmel, D., Eckes, S., & Militello, M. (2010). *Principals teaching the law: 10 legal lessons your teachers must know.* Thousand Oaks, CA: Corwin Press.

Section 504 of the Rehabilitation Act of 1973, 29 U.S.C. § 794: 34 C.F.R. §§ 104 *et seq* (1973).

T.F. v. Fox Chapel Area Sch. Dist., 2013 WL 5936411 (W.D. Pa. 2013).

U.S. Department of Education, National Center for Education Statistics. (2013). Digest of Education Statistics, 2012 (NCES 2014-015), Chapter 2. Retrieved from http://nces.ed.gov/pubs2014/2014015.pdf

U.S. Department of Education, Office for Civil Rights. (2014). *Civil rights data collection: Data snapshot (school discipline).* Retrieved from http://www2.ed.gov/about/ offices/list/ocr/docs/crdc-discipline-snapshot.pdf

U.S. Department of Education, Office of Special Education and Rehabilitative Services. (2010). *Thirty-five years of progress in educating children with disabilities through IDEA.* Washington, D.C. Retrieved from http://www2.ed.gov/ about/offices/list/osers/idea35/history/index.html

U.S. Government Accountability Office (GAO). (2009). *Seclusions and restraints, selected cases of abuse at public and private schools and treatment centers* GAO Report No. 09-719-T), at 7-8. Retrieved from the GAP website: http://www.gao.gov

Yell, M. L. (2016). *The law and special education* (4th ed.). Upper Saddle River, NJ: Pearson.

What Are the Main Federal Entitlements and Protections?

INTRODUCTION FOR FACILITATORS

Since the original passage of the Education for All Handicapped Children Act, which later became the Individuals with Disabilities Education Act (IDEA), in 1975, the federal entitlements and protections for students with disabilities have expanded. Yell (2016) explained, "The history of special education can fairly be characterized as a movement from access to quality and accountability" (p. 60). To that end, it is not enough that you and your colleagues simply be aware of the existence of the rights and protections of students with disabilities; you must also understand what special education law requires and how to apply the law to actual situations arising in your schools.

For example, litigation might have been avoided if a Hawaiian school district had recognized that its decision to hold an Individualized Education Program (IEP) meeting without a student's father because of scheduling difficulties was in violation of the IDEA's requirement to include parents in IEP meetings (*Doug C. v. State of Hawaii Dept. of Ed.*, 2013). Similarly, a Tennessee federal trial court ruled in favor of parents who claimed that their daughter's principal retaliated against them because they asked for accommodations related to their daughter's diabetes (*A.C. v. Shelby Cnty. Bd. of Educ.*, 2013). If the principal had been better versed in the protections of Section 504 of the Rehabilitation Act of 1973 (Section 504) and the Americans with Disabilities Act (ADA), he might have avoided this costly lawsuit.

Many educators may recognize the significance of the IDEA because it is the main federal special education law, but could remain unaware of the importance of Section 504 and ADA, which are federal laws prohibiting disability discrimination. Parents and advocacy organizations are increasingly citing Section 504 and ADA to justify why schools must provide special education and related services for students with disabilities. As a result, districts are facing an increasing number of U.S. Department of Education Office for Civil Rights (OCR) complaints and lawsuits (Yell, 2016).

In light of the need for educators to know about all three federal laws, the purpose of this legal lesson is to explain the general entitlements and protections of the IDEA, Section 504, and ADA. Other legal lessons in this book provide more specific detail about what is required under these laws such as eligibility requirements for special education and related services (Lesson 3) and the procedures that must be followed when disciplining students with disabilities (Lesson 6).

MATERIALS NEEDED

The facilitator should organize the following items prior to the lesson:

- Whiteboard and markers or chalkboard and chalk and prizes for Whiteboard Race (see *Hook*);
- Disability Law Scenario Activity handouts for each participant and Answer Key (see *Activity*);
- Questions typed or written on three handouts (see *Questions for Conversation*);
- Fill-in-the-Blank worksheets and answer key for each participant and answer key (see *Test Your Knowledge*); and
- Optional: Objectives visually displayed (see *Background, Purpose, and Objectives*).

HOOK (5 MINUTES)

To begin the lesson, the facilitator will write the following phrases on a whiteboard or chalkboard:

I______ with D_______ E____________ A_____ (IDEA)
S______ 504 of the R_________ A____________ (Section 504)
F______ A____________ P____________ E____________ (FAPE)
L______ R____________ E____________ (LRE)
A______ with D_______ A_____ (ADA)

Participants will then divide into two teams and form two single-file lines. Facilitators will give the first person in each line the marker/chalk, which will serve as a relay-race baton. Each team will have 2 minutes to take turns filling in one blank on the board at a time. The teams work at the same time, rotating through their lines, racing against the clock and the other team. If a team member gets stuck, the rest of the team can help him or her. The first team to fill in the most accurate blanks within the 2-minute time frame wins. The facilitator may award prizes (e.g., candy) to the winning team.

It is possible that the teams will be unable to fill in most phrases. The facilitator could explain that it is not surprising that they are not familiar with most of the terms, but through today's lesson, they will learn about these three main federal laws and students' legal entitlements. The facilitator could also initiate a conversation with those who knew the terms and ask how they have that knowledge. The correct answers will be discussed in the Test Your Knowledge section of this lesson.

BACKGROUND, PURPOSE, AND OBJECTIVES OF THE LESSON (5 MINUTES)

Next, the facilitator will read the following **Facilitator Script** to the participants or paraphrase the information in their own words (if there is more than one facilitator, you may choose to split the script among them).The facilitator may consider having the Objectives displayed visually so that the participants may refer to them during the lesson.

Facilitator Script

Facilitator: Today's legal lesson will cover the main federal disability laws that apply to school settings. Knowing why these laws exist and what they entail is important. The content of today's legal lesson lays the general foundation so that you can learn more specific details about special education law in future legal lessons. It is similar to needing to know how to add before you learn to multiply. Therefore, we will learn about the general aspects of these laws today, but future legal lessons will include the specifics such as how to determine whether students with disabilities are eligible to receive special education and related services.

Importantly, you should be aware of both federal and state laws regarding special education. The federal law provides the "floor": the minimum services that a school must provide to students with disabilities. State laws can add more expansive requirements for special education services, but cannot provide for less than what federal law requires.

Today, we will primarily focus on the most commonly invoked federal law in Pre-K–12 schools, the Individuals with Disabilities Education Act, which is commonly referred to as IDEA. Enacted in 1975 as the Education for All Handicapped Children Act, IDEA has a variety of protections and entitlements for students with disabilities and their parents. The other two federal laws that we will spend less time discussing are Section 504 of the Rehabilitation Act, commonly called Section 504, and the Americans with Disabilities Act, which is abbreviated as the ADA. The ADA became law in 1990 and extended the reach of Section 504, which also prohibits discrimination against individuals with disabilities by both public and private entities. A key distinguishing factor among the laws is that the IDEA is an *education* law that applies to *students* with disabilities, whereas both ADA and Section 504 are *civil rights* laws applying not only to students, but also to adults within and outside of school settings.

The specific objectives for today's lesson are for you to:

- describe the six main components of the Individuals with Disabilities Education Act (IDEA).
- learn the key features of Section 504 of the Rehabilitation Act (Section 504) and the Americans with Disabilities Act (ADA).
- distinguish the key protections of Section 504 and ADA from the protections of IDEA.

Please feel free to ask questions throughout or at the end of the lesson, and understand that we will revisit these topics in future legal lessons, too.

ACTIVITY (30 MINUTES)

The facilitator will divide the participants into groups of two or three and instruct them to spend the next 25 minutes collaborating to complete the following Disability Law Scenario Activity. First, the participants will each read the first section of the Scenario Activity handout to learn about the IDEA, Section 504, and the ADA. Second, they will discuss the three Disability Law Scenarios. For the final 5 minutes, the facilitators will lead a large-group discussion about the correct responses to the scenarios. To prepare to lead the discussion, the facilitators should review the answer key for the scenarios appears below the Activity.

Disability Law Scenario Activity

First, individually read the information below about the IDEA, Section 504, and the ADA. Then discuss the three scenarios with your group as you apply the law to the scenarios.

The Individuals with Disabilities Education Act (IDEA)

The IDEA is a federal education law that applies to students at public schools in states that accept federal funding (which all states currently do). The IDEA entitles eligible students with disabilities to a variety of protections and entitlements. The IDEA has six main components, including (Yell, 2016):

1. **Zero Reject & Child Find:** Officials of the state educational agencies (SEAs) must locate, assess, and provide services to *all* eligible students with disabilities (20 U.S.C. § 1412[3][A]). This includes children from birth to age 21 enrolled in public school settings as well as nonpublic schools (20 U.S.C. § 1412[a][10][A][I]). Officials of the SEA must identify, locate, and evaluate all students in need of special education and related services or who are suspected of having disabilities (34 C.F.R. § 3000.220). SEA officials cannot

exclude students with disabilities who are eligible to receive special education and related services due to the expense of services or severity of disability (*Timothy W. v. Rochester*, 1989).

2. **Evaluation:** The local educational agency (LEA) must provide evaluations to determine whether students suspected of having IDEA-eligible disabilities are eligible to receive special education and related services. To be eligible, (1) a student must be diagnosed with one of the 13 disabilities listed in the IDEA, and (2) the student's educational performance must be adversely affected due to the disability.
3. **Free Appropriate Public Education (FAPE):** A student who qualifies under the IDEA must receive FAPE, including special education and related services. These services must:
   a. be provided at public expense,
   b. meet standards of the SEA,
   c. include an appropriate education, and
   d. conform to an Individualized Education Program (IEP).
4. **Least Restrictive Environment (LRE):** The LEA must educate students with disabilities in settings with their nondisabled peers to the maximum extent appropriate. Many educators and parents/guardians refer to "inclusion" or "mainstreaming" when determining LRE and student placement. In addition, placement must be individualized for each particular student, and cannot be based solely on diagnoses or what the school has traditionally done for similar students. It also cannot be based on students' disruptive behavior without evidence of a school's attempts to manage students' behavior. Finally, cost cannot be a factor in determining placement, unless the cost is excessive.
5. **Procedural Protections:** The LEA and SEA must follow a variety of procedures to comply with the IDEA's requirements. To ensure that parents/guardians of students with disabilities are aware of the statute's procedural protections, the IDEA requires the LEA to provide a copy of the IDEA procedural safeguards to parents at least once a year (in addition to the initial referral or request for evaluation), upon filing of a complaint, or upon request. If a disagreement arises between the parents and the LEA, the parents/guardians have the option to file a due process complaint.
6. **Involvement of Parents/Guardians:** Under the IDEA, the parents/guardians of students with disabilities have a number of procedural rights in addition to those provided to their children. For example, an LEA must include parents/guardians as part of the IEP team that creates, monitors, and revises a student's IEP at regular intervals. The law requires that parents/guardians must be involved in the decisionmaking process of a child's special education program.

Section 504 and the ADA

Section 504 of the Rehabilitation Act of 1973 (Section 504) prohibits disability discrimination against both students and teachers at public and private schools *that receive governmental funding.* The Americans with Disabilities Act (ADA) prohibits disability discrimination for both students and teachers at *all* public and private schools. Discrimination in violation of Section 504 and the ADA may occur when students with disabilities are excluded from school activities or classes, or receive inferior or different treatment in comparison to nondisabled peers. For example, students may seek protection under Section 504 or the ADA (but not the IDEA) when they encounter either intentional or unintentional discrimination related to nonacademic activities (e.g., students with diabetes who cannot access their insulin during the lunch period) or obstacles to accessing an education (e.g., physical education activities that are inaccessible to students in wheelchairs).

School districts more commonly apply Section 504 rather than the ADA to student disability issues, but courts have ruled that the ADA should be interpreted similarly to Section 504 (Weber, 2010). Students who may not qualify for services under the IDEA, but are in need of reasonable accommodations at school, are provided with a Section 504 Plan instead of an IEP. For example, some students diagnosed with Attention Deficit Hyperactivity Disorder (ADHD) may not qualify for the IDEA because they do not need specialized educational services, but they may qualify for accommodations under Section 504 that are specifically targeted to address learning issues related to ADHD (e.g., allowing a student to take a test with noise-blocking headphones on to reduce auditory distractions).

Generally, accommodations may include, but are not limited to, reduction of classroom distractions, modification of the pace of instruction, and increased time to complete assignments. Under Section 504, eligible students are entitled to receive a FAPE similar to students who qualify under the IDEA; the entitlements and protections, however, are not exactly the same. Students could qualify for accommodations under Section 504 even if their educations were not adversely affected by their disabilities, whereas to be eligible under the IDEA, students' disabilities must adversely affect their educations. Further, under Section 504, schools are not required to involve parents/guardians in educational decisionmaking to the same extent as under the IDEA, yet parents/guardians are still provided with many procedural safeguards under Section 504. To be clear, there are similarities between the IDEA and Section 504, but there are also major differences (e.g., IDEA complaints are filed with the U.S. Office of Special Education Programs [OSEP], whereas Section 504 complaints are filed with the Office of Civil Rights [OCR]).

The Venn diagram below (see Figure 2.1) illustrates the relationship among the three laws. All students who are eligible under the IDEA are also protected by Section 504 and ADA. Some students qualify for protection under Section 504 and ADA, but are NOT eligible for special education under the IDEA. Section 504 only applies to schools that receive governmental funding, whereas ADA applies to all private and public schools.

In sum, Section 504 and ADA are broad laws that protect a greater number of students than the IDEA, which has more stringent eligibility criteria and is limited to children attending school. Additionally, the protections and

Figure 2.1. Disability Law Scenario Activity Venn Diagram

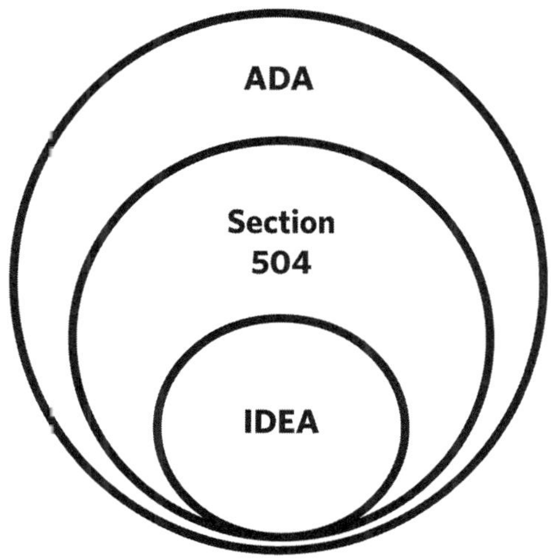

services differ under each of these three laws. Some lawsuits can only be filed under the IDEA, and some can only be filed under Section 504 or the ADA.

Now, as a group, apply the information in the preceding diagram to answer the questions following each scenario.

Disability Law Scenarios

Scenario 1: T.J., a 4th-grader with autism, transfers to a school in Indiana after his family moves from New Jersey. At his first IEP meeting, it is discovered that T.J. had received 20 hours a week of Applied Behavior Analysis (ABA) at his previous school. The special education director tells T.J.'s parents, "ABA is expensive to implement, and no one is trained in the intervention here. I've decided that T.J. will be placed in an autism classroom with other children with autism." When T.J.'s parents protest, the special education director tells them, "Sorry, we just don't have the resources that T.J.'s previous school has. If you disagree with our placement for T.J., your only other option is to move back to New Jersey."

Discuss whether the special education director violated any of the IDEA's six key principles.

Scenario 2: Earlier this year, Valentina had an accident and she lost her ability to hear. Luckily, her cochlear implants allow her to hear well, but she is classified as "hearing-impaired," one of the 13 disabilities covered by the IDEA. She had received As and Bs prior to the accident and has continued to do well in school. Her parents have requested that the school provide 2 hours of one-to-one tutoring to ensure that Valentina continues to do well in school. The principal responded that Valentina is not eligible for special education and related services under the IDEA.

Discuss whether the principal violated any of the IDEA's key six principles.

Scenario 3: Roberto is a kindergarten student who was born with two clubfeet (i.e., his feet were sharply turned inward). Roberto received treatment, and his feet no longer turn inward. However, he still has a lot of pain when he participates in physical activities such as running. Although participation in running is not something that Roberto is graded on, his mother requests that he be excused from running during physical education class.

Do any of the three federal disability laws require the school to accommodate Roberto's mother's request? If so, explain how.

Answer Key for Disability Law Scenarios

Scenario 1: There are four potential violations of the IDEA that your group may have discussed, including:

1. **FAPE**—When the director told T.J.'s parents that ABA was expensive and that they did not have staff trained in that type of intervention, the director violated the requirement under the IDEA that schools provide a FAPE. The IDEA requires that an eligible student's education and related services be based on the student's individual needs. Therefore, cost and/or lack of trained staff are not legal justifications for failing to provide a FAPE.
2. **LRE**—When the director informed T.J.'s parents that T.J. would be placed in the autism classroom, the director violates the IDEA requirement of placement in the LRE. The IDEA requires students to be placed with general education students to the maximum extent appropriate. In T.J.'s situation, the director was going to base his placement solely on his diagnosis of autism, which is inadequate to justify a particular classroom placement.
3. **Procedural Protection**—When the director told T.J.'s parents that their only other option was to move back to New Jersey, it was a violation of the IDEA's requirements of procedural protection. If parents disagree with a district about special education and related services, they can file a due process complaint.
4. **Parental Participation**—The director's unilateral decision that T.J. would not receive ABA intervention, and instead would be placed in the autism classroom, violated the IDEA's requirements regarding parental participation. As members of T.J.'s IEP Team, his parents have the right to be included in activities related to his IEP, and to participate in decisions regarding T.J.'s special education and related services.

Scenario 2: To be eligible, Valentina first must be diagnosed with one of the 13 disabilities listed in the IDEA (see Lesson 3 for discussion of the 13 disabilities). She is classified as hearing impaired which is one of the IDEA's 13 disabilities; therefore, the first criterion is met. Valentina's educational performance must also be adversely affected due to her hearing impairment. However, it is possible that her hearing impairment is not adversely affecting her educational performance, because she continues to do well in school. As a result, Valentina may not be eligible for special education and related services, including the tutoring that her parents have requested. However, the principal must first ensure that Valentina is properly evaluated so the IEP team can base its decisions on objective information, and so all members can participate.

Scenario 3: Yes, both Section 504 and the ADA would apply. Under both of these federal civil rights laws, schools cannot discriminate against students based on a disability. If Roberto was eligible for services under Section 504, the school would need to provide reasonable accommodations, such as being excused from physical education class. We will discuss eligibility determinations more in Lesson 3. The IDEA does not apply in Roberto's situation because his physical disability does not adversely impact his success in school (i.e., his ability to receive a FAPE); therefore, he is not in need of special education and related services under the IDEA.

QUESTIONS FOR CONVERSATION (5 TO 10 MINUTES)

Before the lesson, the facilitator will distribute the following questions to three different participants. The facilitator will direct the selected participants to ask the questions during the lesson or devote time after the activity portion of the lesson for Q-and-A.

1. Under the principle of Child Find, must schools really locate all students with disabilities? Yes. Child Find is a state responsibility mandated by both the IDEA and Section 504. Each state must identify an agency to coordinate Child Find. Most commonly, that task falls to the state public school system and the local school districts.

LEA officials are obligated to locate students with disabilities. Parents do not need to first request that an LEA identify and evaluate a child suspected of having a disability. Therefore, LEA officials must proactively work to locate students who have transferred from other districts, are enrolled in private schools, and/or are homeless.

LEAs meet their Child Find obligations in a variety of ways. For instance, they may publish public notices; respond to referrals from outside agencies such as pediatricians, hospitals, or day care providers; conduct door-to-door visits; or conduct kindergarten screenings. Once LEA officials suspect that a child may be in need of special education services, they must conduct evaluations to determine whether the child is eligible to receive special education and related services.

2. How do the IDEA, the ADA, and Section 504 compare to state laws? Education is a state function, which means that education legislation has traditionally been a responsibility of state government. However, when it comes to providing students with special education and protecting students from disability discrimination, federal laws such as the IDEA, Section 504, and the ADA, are incredibly influential. Because the IDEA is a funding law, states must follow its mandates if they want to receive the federal funding attached to the IDEA's requirements. Currently, all states have chosen to receive that federal funding, so all states must adhere to the IDEA requirements. On the other hand, Section 504 and the ADA are civil rights laws, which means that all states must follow them, although no funding is specifically dependent on compliance.

The federal law requirements are only a minimum. Many states enact statutes and regulations requiring additional entitlements and protections for students with disabilities. For example, the federal government requires states to provide a specified proportion of their the IDEA funding to LEAs. However, some states choose to allocate more than the minimum amount of funding to LEAs. Additionally, some state laws require districts to follow more stringent special education procedures than those that the IDEA requires.

3. Why would parents/guardians file lawsuits under Section 504 or the ADA instead of the IDEA? It may be appealing to file a case under the IDEA because this law provides a number of entitlements and protections to students who qualify for special education and related services. However, if a lawsuit claims that the IDEA was violated, litigants must first have exhausted their administrative remedies. This means that before a person can file an the IDEA lawsuit in state or federal court, she must first file the case in the administrative court system organized by the state educational agency (SEA). States have either one or two required levels of review before an the IDEA lawsuit may be filed in state or federal court.

Conversely, lawsuits alleging Section 504 or the ADA violations may be filed directly in state or federal court. Additionally, more students are covered by Section 504 and the ADA than by the IDEA; therefore, students who have issues that may not be traditionally considered disabilities could still file suit under Section 504 or the ADA. For example, Section 504 litigation has been filed by students who have conditions ranging from food allergies to diabetes to HIV/AIDS. In 2013, in a case where deaf and hearing-impaired students sought word-for-word transcription services, a federal court determined that when a district complies with the IDEA, the district has not necessarily satisfied its Section 504 or the ADA obligations (*K.M. v. Tustin Unified Sch. Dist.*, 2013). This case illustrates how some students who do not prevail in the IDEA lawsuits might still sue successfully under Section 504 or the ADA.

TEST YOUR KNOWLEDGE (10–15 MINUTES)

The facilitator will give each participant the following Fill-in-the-Blank Worksheet to assess whether each individual has mastered the lesson's objectives. Participants will use the answers from the Relay Race that was completed earlier during the Hook to fill in the blanks on the worksheet; however, they should attempt to complete the worksheet without looking at any additional materials. The facilitator will review the participants' responses and follow up with the large group to clarify any of the objectives that were not mastered (for answers to worksheet see the Answer Key and Figure 2.3)

Fill-In-The-Blank Worksheet

First, fill in the blanks:

1. I__________ with D_______ E___________ A_____ (IDEA)
2. S__________ 504 of the R_________ A___________ (Section 504)
3. F__________ A___________ P___________ E___________ (FAPE)
4. L__________ R___________ E___________ (LRE)
5. A__________ with D_______ A_____ (ADA)

Second, use the above abbreviations (e.g., IDEA) to complete the following sentences. Most of the abbreviations will be used more than once.

1. ________________________ is a federal law requiring schools to provide children with disabilities a free appropriate public education (FAPE) in the least restrictive environment (LRE).
2. Six main components of __________ are:
a. Zero Reject
b. Evaluation
c. Free Appropriate Public Education (FAPE)
d. Least Restrictive Environment (LRE)
e. Procedural Safeguards
f. Parental Participation
3. Zero Reject is one of the six main components of__________, which requires schools to provide a FAPE to *every* child with a disability who is eligible for special education and related services.
4. Evaluation is one of the six main components of __________. Schools must conduct a full and individual evaluation of a student before the student is provided special education and related services.
5. ________________________ is one of the six main components of the IDEA. Students who qualify under IDEA must be given an education at public expense, meeting state standards. This includes preschool through secondary school, and educators must conform to the student's Individualized Education Program (IEP).
6. ________________________ is one of the six main components of the IDEA, mandating that children with disabilities are to be taught with children without disabilities to the maximum extent appropriate.
7. Procedural Safeguards is one of the six main components of __________. For example, parents/guardians must be provided with reasonable notice before any major changes in the student's education. Also,

Figure 2.2. Test Your Knowledge Venn Diagram

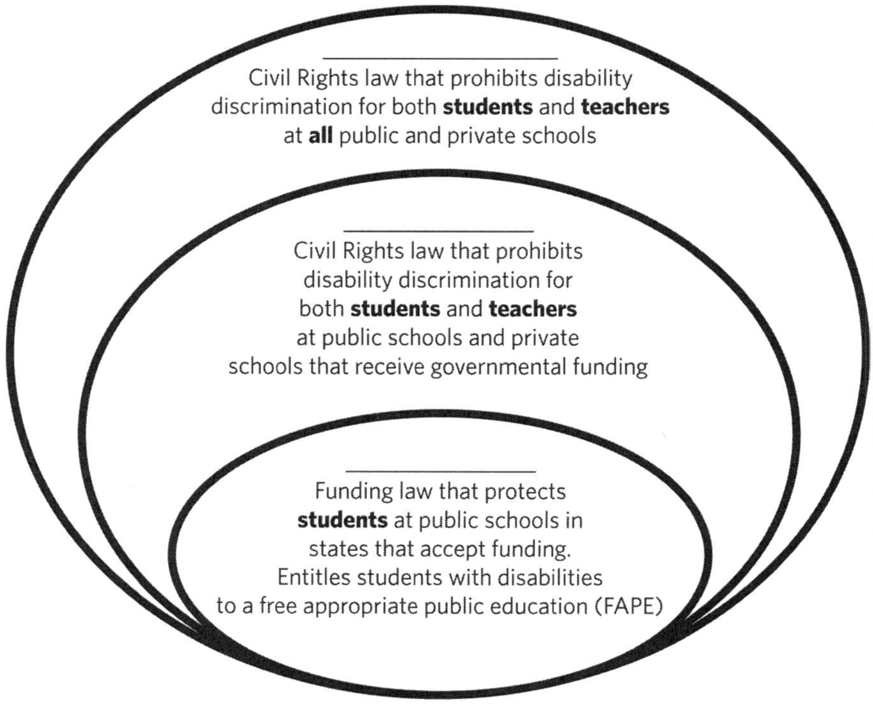

parents/guardians must be provided with an opportunity to consent prior to a student being evaluated.

8. Parental Participation is one of the six main components of ___________. Parents/guardians have independent, enforceable rights and must be provided with an opportunity to be a member of their child's IEP team.
9. Fill in the blanks in the Venn diagram shown below (see Figure 2.2):

Answer Key for the Fill-in-the-Blank Worksheet

First, fill in the blanks:

1. Individuals with Disabilities Education Act (IDEA)
2. Section 504 of the Rehabilitation Act (Section 504)
3. Free Appropriate Public Education (FAPE)
4. Least Restrictive Environment (LRE)
5. Americans with Disabilities Act (ADA)

Second, use the above abbreviations (e.g., IDEA) to complete the following sentences. Most of the abbreviations will be used more than once.

1. IDEA
2. IDEA

Figure 2.3: Answer Key Venn Diagram

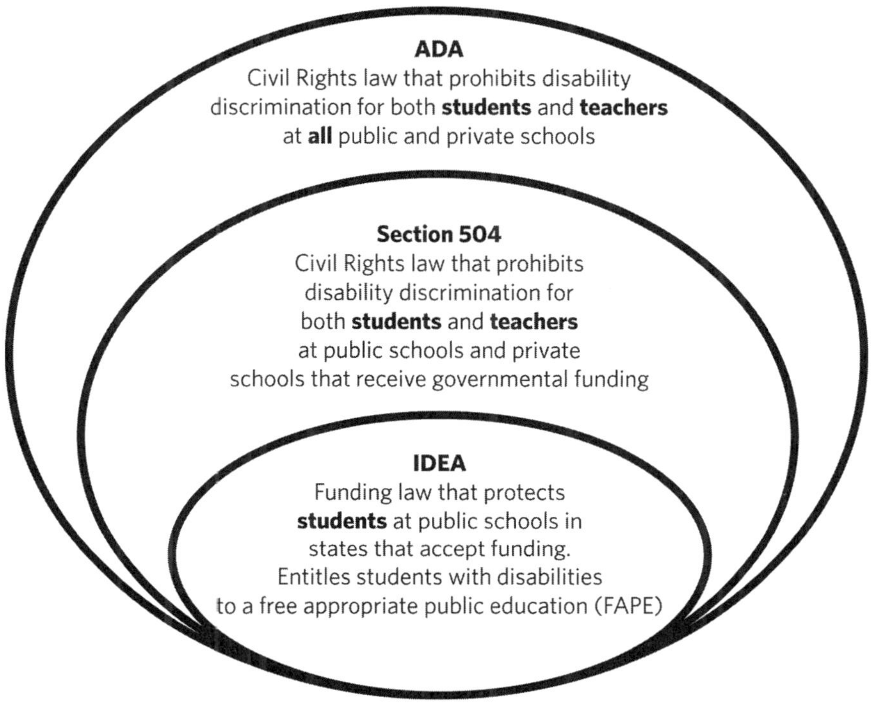

3. IDEA
4. IDEA
5. FAPE
6. LRE
7. IDEA
8. IDEA

ADDITIONAL RESOURCES

NICHY (National Dissemination Center for Children with Disabilities), The Americans with Disabilities Act. http://nichcy.org/laws/ada

NICHY (National Dissemination Center for Children with Disabilities), Section 504 of the Rehabilitation Act of 1973. http://nichcy.org/laws/section504

PACER, ADA Q&A: Back to School. http://www.pacer.org/publications/adaqa/school.asp

Russo, C. J., & Osborne, A. G. (2008). *Essential concepts & school-based cases in special education law.* Thousand Oaks, CA: Corwin Press.

U.S. Department of Education Office for Civil Rights, The Americans with Disabilities Act. http://www2.ed.gov/about/offices/list/ocr/docs/hq9805.html

U.S. Department of Education Office for Civil Rights, Protecting Students with Disabilities. http://www2.ed.gov/about/offices/list/ocr/504faq.html

U.S. Department of Justice Civil Rights Division Information and Technical Assistance on the Americans with Disabilities Act. (2009). http://www.ada.gov/

REFERENCES

A.C. v. Shelby Cnty. Bd. of Ed., 711 F.3d 687 (6th Cir. 2013).

Americans with Disabilities Act, 42 U.S.C. § 12101.

Doug C. v. State of Hawaii Dep't. of Ed., 720 F.3d 1038 (9th Cir. 2013).

Individuals with Disabilities Education Act, 20 U.S.C. §§ 1400 *et seq.*, 34 C.F.R. §§ 200 *et seq.*

K.M. v. Tustin Unified Sch. Dist., 725 F.3d 1088 (9th Cir., 2013).

Section 504 of the Rehabilitation Act of 1973, 29 U.S.C. § 794: 34 C.F.R. §§ 104 *et seq.* (1973).

Timothy W. v. Rochester, 875 F.2d 954 (1st Cir. 1989).

Weber, M. C. (2010). A new look at Section 504 and the ADA in special education cases. *Texas Journal on Civil Liberties and Civil Rights, 16,* 1–27.

Yell, M. L. (2016). *Law and special education* (4th ed.). Upper Saddle River, NJ: Pearson.

Who Is Eligible for Special Education?

INTRODUCTION FOR FACILITATORS

A central question in special education litigation is "who is protected" under current federal special education laws. The issue of student eligibility under existing special education laws is often an area of dispute between educators and the parents/guardians of students with disabilities. Today's school officials sometimes fail to follow proper policies and procedures related to student eligibility detailed in special education laws. In a growing number of instances, for example, courts have held the school district legally responsible for improperly finding a student ineligible for special education and related services (Yell, 2016). In one case, a court ruled that a substance-abusing 9th-grader was eligible for special education and related services and the school district was liable for tuition reimbursement, based on the district's delayed evaluation and misidentification of the student's eligibility under the Individuals with Disabilities Education Act (IDEA) (*New Paltz Central Sch. Dist. v. St. Pierre*, 2004).

Legal issues involving student eligibility are especially important to the parents/guardians of students with disabilities. According to the U.S. Supreme Court, a student's special education eligibility entitles parents to "meaningful input into all decisions affecting their child's education and the right to seek review of any decisions they think appropriate" (*Honig v. Doe*, 1988).

This lesson clarifies the current eligibility requirements for students with disabilities under federal law, which are often, though not always, mirrored in individual states' laws (Garda, 2004). There are three primary federal laws developed to legally protect and enhance the rights of students with disabilities: the Individuals with Disabilities Education Act (IDEA, 2006), Section 504 of the Rehabilitation Act (1973) (Section 504), and the Americans with Disabilities Act (1990) (ADA). All three of these federal laws vary in terms of student eligibility criteria.

The IDEA legally guarantees students with disabilities a Free Appropriate Public Education (FAPE) individualized to their specific needs (20 U.S.C. § 1412[a][1]). Prior to receiving special education and related services under IDEA, students must first satisfy the definition of a child with a disability.

There are three components to the IDEA's "child with a disability" definition:

1. The student must meet the requirements of one or more of the 13 eligibility categories under the IDEA, including:
   a. Autism,
   b. Deaf-blindness,
   c. Deafness,
   d. Hearing impairment,
   e. Intellectual disability,
   f. Multiple disabilities,
   g. Orthopedic impairments,
   h. Other health impairment,
   i. Emotional disturbance,
   j. Specific learning disability,
   k. Speech or language impairment,
   l. Traumatic brain injury, and
   m. Visual impairment, including blindness.
2. The student must require special education and related services based on the eligible disability.
3. The eligible disability must "adversely affect" the student's academic performance.

Under the IDEA, both individual states and local school districts also have the discretion to use the term "developmental delay" with children who are 3 through 9 years of age, if they experience developmental delays in one or more of the following areas: physical development, cognitive development, communication development, social or emotional development, or adaptive development.

It is possible for a student to have a disability, but not need special education or related services and consequently not qualify as eligible under the IDEA. For example, a student may have a disability, such as an orthopedic impairment (e.g., clubfoot), but if this particular physical disability does not adversely affect the student's ability to participate and academically or otherwise succeed in school, then that student would not qualify for services under the IDEA.

Unlike the IDEA, both Section 504 and the ADA are federal civil rights laws that apply to students as well as nonstudent adults. Although Section 504 and the ADA have some differences (see Lesson 2), their definition of disability is identical. Before receiving protection under either Section 504 or the ADA, a student must have a disability, which is defined as:

1. a physical or medical impairment which substantially limits one or more of such person's major life activities,
2. a record of such an impairment, or

3. is regarded as having such an impairment (29 U.S.C. § 706[7][B]; 42 U.S.C. § 12102 [2]).

More specifically, Section 504 and ADA regulations define a physical impairment in the following way:

> [A]ny physiological disorder or condition, cosmetic disfigurement, or anatomical loss affecting one or more of the following body systems: neurological; musculoskeletal; special sense organs, respiratory, including speech organs; cardiovascular; reproductive, digestive, genito-urinary; hemic and lymphatic; skin and endocrine (Section 504 Regulations, 34 C.F.R. § 104.3 [j][2][i]).

Section 504 regulations define a person with a mental impairment as:

> Any mental or psychological disorder, such as mental retardation, organic brain syndrome, emotional or mental illness, and specific learning disabilities (34 C.F.R. § 104.3 [j][2][i]).

Finally, Section 504 defines substantial life activities as "functions, such as caring for one's self, performing manual tasks, walking, seeing, hearing, breathing, learning, and working" (34 C.F.R. § 104.3[j][2][ii]).

MATERIALS NEEDED

The facilitator should collect the following materials:

- Who Is Eligible Chart handout for each participant, and facilitator script (see *Background, Purpose, and Objectives*);
- Game show materials including facilitator script, prizes, 5 green signs stating "ELIGIBLE" and 5 red signs stating "NOT ELIGIBLE," handout or other visual display of the 3 scenarios, a sign stating "APPLAUSE PLEASE!," and the answer key to the scenarios;
- Copies of the quiz for each participant (see *Test Your Knowledge*), and the answer key; and
- Optional: Objectives visually displayed (see *Background, Purpose, and Objectives*).

HOOK (10 MINUTES)

To begin this lesson, the facilitator will ask the participants to view the 6-minute video linked here http://www.youtube.com/watch?v=XncgzTGEzZY. This video details some of the most common questions regarding special education eligibility rules. It was created for parents in New Jersey, but it applies to all states. After the video is over, ask the participants to share their thoughts about the video with other participants.

BACKGROUND, PURPOSE, AND OBJECTIVES OF THE LESSON (5 MINUTES)

Next, the facilitators will read the following **Facilitator Script** to the participants or paraphrase the information in their own words (if there is more than one facilitator, you may choose to split the script among them). While reading the script, the Facilitator will distribute the "Who Is Eligible Chart" handout (Table 3.1) to each participant. The facilitator should consider having the objectives displayed visually so that the participants can refer to them during the lesson.

Facilitator: Today's lesson will discuss which students are eligible to receive special education or related services based on their disability. I'm handing out a chart that outlines three federal laws that clarify how to determine whether a particular student has a disability. You will notice that Section 504 and the ADA's eligibility requirements are the same, whereas the IDEA's eligibility requirements differ. If a student qualifies under the IDEA, the school may be responsible for providing more or different services than if a student qualifies under Section 504 or the ADA. For example, a student who qualifies under the IDEA will be eligible to receive an Individualized Education Program (IEP), whereas a student who qualifies under Section 504 will be eligible to receive a Section 504 Plan. Therefore, it is important for you to know which of your students qualify for which type(s) of services. As you may know, the purpose of Section 504 is to ensure that students with disabilities are not discriminated against and have access to an education, wherea, the purpose of IDEA is to ensure that students with disabilities have a free appropriate public education, also known as FAPE.

The specific objectives for today's lesson are:

1. Explore how disability is defined differently under the three leading special education laws: the Individuals with Disabilities Education Act (IDEA), Section 504 of the Rehabilitation Act (Section 504), and the Americans with Disabilities Act (ADA).
2. Apply legal requirements to student scenarios to determine student eligibility.

Table 3.1. "Who Is Eligible" Chart Handout—A Comparison of IDEA, Section 504, and ADA Eligibility

IDEA	Section 504	ADA
Eligibility criteria:	Eligibility criteria:	Eligibility criteria:
For students aged 0–21 prior to and in elementary and secondary education, who are determined by a multidisciplinary team to be eligible within one or more of 13 specific disability categories and who need special education and related services. Categories include autism, deafness, deaf-blindness, hearing impairments, mental retardation, multiple disabilities, orthopedic impairments, other health impairments, serious emotional disturbance, specific learning disabilities, speech or language impairments, traumatic brain injury, and visual impairments.	Any person who: (1) has a physical or mental impairment that substantially limits one or more major life activities; (2) has a record of such an impairment; or (3) is regarded as having such an impairment. Major life activities include walking, seeing, hearing, speaking, breathing, learning, working, caring for oneself, and performing manual tasks.	Any individual with a disability who: (1) has a physical or mental impairment that substantially limits one or more life activities; (2) has a record of such impairment; or (3) is regarded as having such an impairment. Further, the person must be qualified for the program, service, or job.

Source: Disability Rights Education & Defense Fund (DREDF) (www.dredf.org).

ACTIVITY (30 MINUTES)

Game Show Activity

The facilitator will introduce a game show called "You Make the Call." The facilitator will divide the participants into four teams that will compete to get the most correct answers based on the following scenarios. The facilitator will read the scenarios aloud; then the teams will discuss the scenarios and decide if the student in the scenario is eligible for special education services. A designated team leader will hold up either a green sign that says "ELIGIBLE" or a red sign that says "NOT ELIGIBLE." Prizes (e.g., candy) will be awarded to the winning team of participants.

Facilitator: Welcome, everyone! You are the lucky contestants on the award-winning game show "You Make the Call." First, please divide into four teams *[the facilitator could also have the teams assigned prior to the lesson].*

Facilitator: I'm going to read three scenarios involving students who may or may not be eligible for special education and related services under one of three current federal disability laws: the Individuals with Disabilities Education Act (IDEA), Section 504 of the Rehabilitation Act (Section 504), or the Americans with Disabilities Act (ADA). After I read these three scenarios, your teams will discuss and determine whether the student is eligible or ineligible for special education under IDEA, Section 504, or the ADA *[the facilitator holds up the green sign indicating eligible and the red sign indicating not eligible]*. After each team has made a decision, a designated team leader will hold up either the green "ELIGIBLE" sign or the red "NOT ELIGIBLE" sign. The team with the most correct responses wins.

Participants: What fabulous prizes can we win?

Facilitator: *[Explain what prizes you have brought, then hold up a sign that reads, "APPLAUSE PLEASE!"]*

Participants: *[Clap]*

Facilitator: Before we get started, let me make sure everyone has some important background information involving student eligibility requirements of who is protected under the ADA, Section 504, and the IDEA. You have been given an eligibility chart that outlines the requirements. Please review that chart, then raise your hand when you are done reading.

Facilitator: *[Waits until the participants have reviewed the chart.]*

Facilitator: Okay, is everyone ready to win some fabulous prizes?

Facilitator: *[Hold up the sign that reads, "APPLAUSE PLEASE!"]*

Participants: *[Clap.]*

Facilitator: Great. Before we get started, let's analyze the first scenario together. Our first scenario involves Suzanne *[Now, read Scenario 1. Each participant should have a copy of each of the three scenarios, too]*.

Student Special Education Eligibility Scenarios

Scenario 1: Suzanne, a 16-year-old high school student, was recently involved in an accident where she lost significant hearing in both ears. Suzanne had an operation where she received cochlear implants, which have greatly improved her hearing, but she continues to be labeled "hearing-impaired" at her high school. Prior to the accident, Suzanne received mostly As and Bs on her report card. After the accident, her grades have declined slightly but are still mostly As and Bs. Suzanne's parents asked the school to provide 2 hours of individual tutoring based on her hearing impairment. Is Suzanne currently eligible for special education and related services under the IDEA, Section 504, and/or the ADA?

Scenario 2: Lucas, a 13-year-old middle school student, has been diagnosed with chronic fatigue syndrome (CFS). Some of Lucas's symptoms include numbness, dizziness, and migraine headaches. Occasionally Lucas experiences some muscle pain and temporary loss of short-term memory. While in class, Lucas is often tired, which impacts his ability to fully concentrate and participate in school-related activities. Lucas's grades have been declining steadily over the past 2 years (from mainly Bs to Cs and Ds). Based on an initial evaluation by the school district, Lucas was found ineligible for special education and related services under the IDEA. His parents, however, are now asking the school whether Lucas is eligible for Section 504. What do you think?

Scenario 3: Ginger, a 9-year-old elementary school student, was recently diagnosed with both attention deficit hyperactivity disorder (ADHD) and autism. Since she entered the 3rd grade last year, Ginger's grades have fallen dramatically. She used to receive mainly Bs and Cs and now is receiving Ds and one F. Ginger's parents desperately want the school to place her in a classroom with as few distractions as possible. Is Ginger eligible for special education and related services under the IDEA or Section 504?

Answer Key for Student Special Education Eligibility Scenarios

Scenario 1: (Field responses from the participants, then clarify.) Determining whether a student is eligible under the IDEA is not always an easy task. We know that hearing impairment is one of the 13 potential eligibility disability categories. In Suzanne's situation, because she is hearing-impaired, the first criterion of being a "student with a disability" has been met. However, we need to meet all three criteria to be eligible under the IDEA. The second criterion is: "The student must require special education and related services based on the eligible disability." Since Suzanne is able to hear with her cochlear implants, nothing suggests that she requires special education and related services. So the second criterion for eligibility is not met. The third criterion for the IDEA eligibility requires that Suzanne's educational performance be "adversely affected" based on her disability. This requirement is often a controversial area where parents and school officials disagree. In Suzanne's case, her grades have remained relatively stable after the accident, and it does not appear that her education was adversely affected by her hearing impairment. Two of the three required criteria to find eligibility under the IDEA have not been met; therefore, Suzanne is determined **NOT ELIGIBLE** for special education and related services under the IDEA.

Scenario 2: [Field responses from the participants, then clarify.] In this scenario, Lucas is considered **ELIGIBLE** for accommodations under Section 504. His chronic fatigue syndrome (CFS) is a condition that can support eligibility under Section 504. Specifically, Lucas has a physical or mental impairment (i.e., CFS), which substantially limits one or more major life activities (e.g., concentrating and sleeping).

Scenario 3: [Field responses from the Participants, then clarify.] The correct answer is that Ginger is **ELIGIBLE** under both the IDEA and Section 504. This is a fairly tricky student eligibility scenario. Students with ADHD may also receive accommodations under Section 504. Ginger was also diagnosed with autism, which is one of the 13 disability categories under the IDEA. The results of Ginger's evaluation reveal that her disabilities have adversely affected her educational performance because her grades have significantly decreased.

Facilitator: Excellent! It looks like this team *(point to appropriate team)* is the winner!

QUESTIONS FOR CONVERSATION (5–10 MINUTES)

Before the lesson, the facilitator will distribute the following questions to three different participants. The facilitator can ask the selected participants to ask the questions during the Legal Lesson, or may devote a time after the Activity portion of the lesson for Q-and-A.

1. *What happens when a school determines that a student is not eligible for special education services under the IDEA?* The school system must inform the parents/guardians in writing and explain specifically why the child has been found "not eligible." Additionally, the parents/guardians must be provided information regarding what next steps may be taken if they disagree with the school system's decision.

2. *Does a student need to be academically failing courses in order to be eligible for special education services under the IDEA?* No. The law states exactly the opposite. According to IDEA regulation 300.101(c), the school must provide special education to a child with a disability "even though the child has not failed or been retained in a course or grade, and is advancing from grade to grade. Failing classes is not required to establish eligibility for special education and related services under IDEA. There are three components to the IDEA's "child with a disability" definition. These three components are: (1) the student must meet the requirements of one or more of the 13 eligibility categories under the IDEA; (2) the student must require special education and related services based on the eligible disability; and (3) the eligible disability must "adversely affect" the student's academic performance.

3. *Are students previously eligible under the IDEA but who no longer qualify, automatically eligible for Section 504 special education services?* It depends. Students who are no longer eligible for special education and related services under the IDEA may qualify for Section 504 accommodations if these students continue experiencing difficulties academically in the school environment. Specifically, Section 504 eligibility is defined as a physical or medical impairment that substantially limits one or more of a person's major life activities and where there is a documented record of this impairment.

At the end of the presentations, the facilitator will hand out or visually display the following quiz for participants to discuss among the entire group.

TEST YOUR KNOWLEDGE (5–10 MINUTES)

The facilitators will distribute the following true-false quiz to assess whether each participant has mastered the objectives of the lesson.

True-False Questions For Participants

1. A student identified with one or more of the current 13 eligibility disability categories automatically qualifies for special education and related services under the IDEA.
2. Local school districts have the discretion to use the term "developmental delay" with children who are 3 through 9 years of age, if the student experiences developmental delays in the areas of physical, cognitive, or emotional development.
3. Under Section 504, eligibility is limited to students with physical impairments that substantially limit one or more major life activities.
4. Similar to the IDEA, Section 504 students are required to have an IEP.
5. School districts may be held liable for tuition reimbursement if they delay evaluation and/or misidentify a student's eligibility under the IDEA.

Answer Key for the Test Your Knowledge True-False Quiz

1. **False.** Being identified with one or more of the current 13 IDEA disability categories is only one of three criteria necessary to become eligible under the IDEA. In addition to being identified with an IDEA-eligible disability, the student must require special education and related services based on that particular disability, and the disability must "adversely affect" the student's academic performance.
2. **True.**
3. **False.** Students eligible for Section 504 may have physiological disorders or conditions, including cosmetic disfigurement, or anatomical loss affecting one or more of the following body systems: neurological; musculoskeletal; special sense organs, respiratory, including speech organs; cardiovascular; reproductive, digestive, genito-urinary; hemic and lymphatic; skin and endocrine.
4. **False.** Students eligible under Section 504 are not required to have an IEP. Instead, eligible students usually have a designated Section 504 accommodation plan.
5. **True.** A 2004 court ruling (*New Paltz Central Sch. Dist. v. St. Pierre*, 2004) held that a substance-abusing 9th-grader was eligible for special education and related services, and the district was held liable for tuition

reimbursement based on the district's delayed evaluation and misidentification of the student's eligibility under the IDEA.

ADDITIONAL RESOURCES

National Center for Learning Disabilities. http://www.ncld.org/ disability/learn-ld -laws. Wrightslaw. http://www.wrightslaw.com/info/elig.index.htm

REFERENCES

Americans with Disabilities Act, 42 U.S.C. § 12101. (1990).

Garda, R.A. (2004). Untangling eligibility requirements under the Individuals with Disabilities Education Act (IDEA). *Missouri Law Review, 69*(2), 441–512.

Honig v. Doe, 484 U.S. 305 (1988).

Individuals with Disabilities Education Act, 20 U.S.C. §§ 1400, et seq., 34 C.F.R. §§ 200 et seq. (2006).

New Paltz Central Sch. Dist. v. St. Pierre, 307 F.Supp.2d 394 (2nd Cir. 2004).

Section 504 of the Rehabilitation Act of 1973, 29 U.S.C. § 794; 34 C.F.R. § 104, et seq. (1973).

Yell, M. L. (2016). *The law and special education* (4th ed.).Boston, MA: Pearson.

How Can We Ensure an Appropriate IEP?

INTRODUCTION FOR FACILITATORS

Once a student with a disability has gone through the referral, identification, and eligibility processes, under the Individuals with Disabilities Education Act (IDEA), it is time to develop their Individualized Education Program (IEP). The goal of an IEP is to outline the special education and related services that are specially designed to confer an educational benefit on the child (*Bd. of Educ. of Hendrick Hudson Sch. Dist.*, 1982). An IEP team, which includes both parents/guardians and educators, develops an IEP to confer appropriate education, services, and placement for a child (20 U.S.C. § 1414[d][1][A][i][IV]). Parents/guardians and educators play important roles as members of the IEP team that determines the child's free appropriate public education (FAPE).

Problems can arise at various stages of the IEP development and implementation process that can lead to litigation. For example, if the parents/guardians of a student with a disability disagree about the programs and services that are included in the IEP, the disagreement may lead to litigation (Logsdon, n.d.; Shuran & Roblyer, 2012). Even when the parents/guardians agree with the IEP, if the school district fails to properly implement it, they may sue. Examples of improper implementation include the school district's failure to provide the specially designed instruction to a student; its failure to make adaptations or modifications needed for student testing; or its failure to deliver related services such as speech therapy, occupational therapy, or physical therapy specified by the IEP (Logsdon, n.d.). Moreover, even when the IEP is being implemented as written, if the programs and services do not actually convey an educational benefit on the student, Free Appropriate Public Education (FAPE) is denied and litigation is possible. Lawsuits over FAPE issues are the most prevalent type of special education–related litigation in the United States (Shuran & Roblyer, 2012).

To ensure an appropriate IEP, educators should: (1) follow the timelines in IDEA and any applicable state law; (2) invite the appropriate people—general education teacher, special education teacher, parents/guardians, local education agency (LEA) representative, and an individual to interpret the evaluation results, such as a psychologist—to participate on the IEP team; (3) address all required elements of the IEP; (4) formalize the IEP (20 U.S.C. § 1414 d] [1]); and (5) implement the IEP as written. These steps will be discussed in this chapter.

MATERIALS NEEDED

- Several copies of the skit script (see *Hook*);
- Table and chairs set up for the IEP role-play activity;
- FAPE PowerPoint (see this book's website);
- Packets for IEP development role-play activity (see *Activity*);
- Objective/goal-setting worksheet for each participant (see *Background, Purpose, and Objectives of the Lesson*);
- Questions for conversation on note cards (see *Questions for Conversation*); and
- Scenarios for the Educational Benefit Game Show and paper and pens for each participant (see *Test Your Knowledge*).
- Optional: Objectives visually displayed (see *Background, Purposes, and Objectives*)

BACKGROUND, PURPOSE, AND OBJECTIVES OF THE LESSON

Next, the facilitator will read the following facilitator script, or discuss the topics raised in the script in another way with the participants. It would be useful to display the objectives visually for the participants to refer to during the lesson.

Facilitator Script

While we know that special education cases make up the bulk of K–12 education litigation, it is important to note that the largest share of special education cases are comprised of FAPE legal challenges (Zirkel & Manchin, 2012). These lawsuits, typically brought by parents/guardians, contest either the substantive or procedural elements of FAPE or both (Zirkel & Manchin, 2012). Although school districts win the vast majority of these cases, when districts fail to follow IDEA's procedures and substantive requirements, parents/guardians often prevail. For example, in a substantive FAPE case involving a child with autism attending a private school, a court held that the district's IEP did not afford FAPE because the parents were providing an additional 2 hours of instruction each night, and this instruction was required for the child to receive a meaningful educational benefit. The court concluded that the school needed to provide more services to the child (*New Milford Bd. of Educ. v. C.R.*, 2011).

In another case involving a student with multiple disabilities, the court ruled that the school district denied the child a meaningful educational benefit because his academic skills regressed in reading, writing, and mathematics during 2nd grade, in part due to the district's failure to provide services promised in the IEP. The court noted that the child had the potential to make significant gains in these subjects with appropriate services (*Woods v. Northport Pub. Sch.*, 2012). In a third case, a court found a procedural violation of IDEA when a school district failed to perform a cognitive evaluation or an assistive technology evaluation of a student with a congenital condition. The court noted that these assessments are necessary to develop appropriate educational goals for the student, so she was denied FAPE in the program provided by the district (*K.I. v. Montgomery Pub. Sch.*, 2011).

The specific objectives for today's lesson are for you to be able to:

1. Understand the legal significance of IEP meetings;
2. Explain the key components of an IEP; and
3. Identify situations where a student with a disability is possibly being denied FAPE.

HOOK (10 MINUTES)

Next, the facilitator will choose seven participants to act out a skit portraying an adversarial IEP meeting that ends with the parents/guardians threatening a lawsuit. If there are fewer than seven willing participants, you may have individuals fill more than one role. The facilitator should narrate the skit.

IEP Meeting Script

Special Education Director, Teacher, Psychologist, Special Education Teacher, Mother, and Assistant Principal are seated around a table. The narrator is standing at the side of the table.

Narrator: The participants in today's meeting are supposed to discuss and finalize an Individualized Education Program, or IEP, for Alexa, who is a 1st-grade student with autism. According to the Individuals with Disabilities Education Act (IDEA), Alexa's parents must be included in the decision-making process about Alexa's education, related services, and placement. Therefore, Alexa's mother is at the meeting as part of the IEP team. At the conclusion of the IEP meeting, Alexa's mother and the school are to sign the IEP, which becomes a legally binding contract. However, as you will see, determining what Alexa's education should include is not always easy.

Director of Special Education: Welcome, everyone. As you know, today we are having this meeting to determine Alexa's IEP goals, services, and placement.

Let's start by having everyone introduce themselves. I'll start by telling you that I'm the Director of Special Education.

Teacher: I'm Alexa's homeroom teacher. I really don't think I need to be here. I just met Alexa this year, and I don't think I have much to contribute to this meeting. Plus, the substitute teacher who was supposed to cover for me never showed up, so I really need to get back to my classroom.

Psychologist: I'm the school psychologist. I have had the opportunity to meet with Alexa and conduct some testing.

Special Education Teacher: I'm Alexa's special education teacher, and I have been working with her for a year. She is a delightful child. She met her IEP goals last year in reading but not in math. I'm looking forward to talking about her successes and challenges as we set new goals for her.

Assistant Principal: I'm the assistant principal. Principal Toobusy couldn't be here today, so I am filling in for him.

Alexa's Mother (speaking in a forceful tone of voice): I'm Alexa's mother and I'd like to talk about her educational progress. I think Alexa needs a full-time aide to be successful in math because what you provided last year didn't work!

Director of Special Education (speaking in an annoyed tone of voice): It isn't time to make suggestions about services yet. We need to hear from the school psychologist about the results of Alexa's testing and from her teachers about her educational progress last year.

Alexa's Mother (speaking in an annoyed tone): I know that I am an equal member of this IEP team. Why can't I speak first?

Psychologist (speaking in a professional tone): I think the information I have to share will provide a good context for our meeting. I'll start by discussing Alexa's progress in reading and then in math.

Narrator: The psychologist shares Alexa's test scores in reading and math.

Director of Special Education: Based on the information shared by the psychologist, we recommend that Alexa continue with her current reading placement, and that she attend a supported math classroom at her grade level that is cotaught by a general education teacher and a special education teacher.

Alexa's Mother (speaking in an annoyed tone): I told you, Alexa needs an individual aide in math to be successful. If you aren't going to listen to my suggestions, I will leave this meeting and file a due process hearing lawsuit instead. *(Stands up and walks out of the meeting.)*

Next, the facilitator will lead a discussion about the problems with the scenario portrayed in the skit and give an overview of the legal requirements of FAPE using the PowerPoint presentation available on this book's website. The presentation gives a brief overview of FAPE and the Rowley legal test. Courts use the Rowley test to determine if the school provided FAPE. The Rowley test asks two main questions:

1. Has the state or LEA complied with IDEA's procedural requirements?
2. Is the IEP reasonably calculated to enable the child to receive educational benefits?

ACTIVITY (25 MINUTES)

For the IEP annual review role-play, the facilitator will arrange the participants into one or more IEP planning teams and have each person assume a role on the team. After instructions are given, each IEP team will be given a packet that includes: (1) IEP meeting notice, (2) IEP meeting agenda, (3) student's IEP, and (4) information for each individual participant about his or her role. Participants will have 5 minutes to review their packets and prepare for the upcoming IEP meeting. After 5 minutes, each small group will conduct the role-play (10 minutes).

After the role-play, the facilitator will lead a discussion (10 minutes) about it by asking the following questions: What struck you? What did you learn about the IEP process? What questions do you still have?

IEP Annual Review Role-Play

Facilitator: Convening a meeting to review an IEP is a foundational element of IDEA. In reviewing an IEP to determine if the school has provided a free appropriate public education (FAPE), courts ask two primary questions:

1. Has the school complied with the IDEA's procedural requirements?
2. Is the IEP reasonably calculated to enable the child to receive educational benefits?

We are going to participate in a role-play to look at the procedural and substantive aspects of FAPE for a high school student with attention deficit disorder (ADD). We'll assign roles and give you time to review the materials before we begin.

The Scenario

In this role-play, the IEP team for "Lucas" is meeting to discuss his progress during his 9th-grade year as part of the annual review process. Lucas has ADD and has been receiving special education accommodations and services for several years. The team consists of the special education director for the LEA, the high school principal, his parents, a general education teacher, a special education teacher, and a psychologist. Each participant should review the documents and then assume a character role based on the information provided.

Assign individuals to key roles and provide 5 minutes for them to review the information. Then provide 10 minutes for the role-play and 10 minutes for the reflection questions.

Individualized Education Program Meeting Notice

Parent/Guardian: Mr. & Mrs. Parent
Mailing Address: 1111 Main Street, Everytown U.S.A.

You are invited to attend an Individualized Education Program (IEP) team meeting for your child on Monday, 10 a.m., Room 200, Everytown High School. The purpose of this meeting is an annual review of your child's IEP. We will consider existing records, academic assessments, parent input, and student observations during this meeting. Your participation and input in this meeting are essential in arriving at decisions about your child's education.

The following individuals have been invited:

Everytown High School Principal, Manuel Manager
School Psychologist, Tara Therapist
General Education Teacher, Edith Educator
Special Education Teacher, Ian Instructor
Student, Lucas

You may invite other individuals who possess expertise or knowledge necessary for the development of your child's IEP.

A copy of your Parents' Rights/Procedural Safeguards and the meeting agenda are attached to this notice.

—Debbie Director,
Director of Special Education,
Everytown Consolidated School District

Annual IEP Meeting Agenda

1. Introduction of IEP team members
2. Procedural safeguards review
3. Reports on present levels of performance
    a. General Education Teacher grades
    b. Special Education Specialist—observation
    c. School Psychologist
4. Family report on present levels of performance
5. Progress on previous goals—IEP team members
6. Current goals—IEP team members
7. Placement, supports, and services
    Frequency, location, & duration of services

Supplementary aids and services, and assistive technology
General education accommodations and modifications

8. Offer of Free Appropriate Education made by school

Individualized Education Program for Lucas (Excerpts)

Lucas is a 9th-grade student with Attention Deficit Disorder.

Strengths:	Areas of Concern:
Upbeat personality	Easily distracted
Motivated by success	Rushes to finish work
Good technology skills	Difficulty writing paragraphs
	Trouble proofreading

Present Levels of Educational Performance:

General Curriculum Area(s) affected by this student's disabilities: English Language Arts (ELA), Social Studies

How does the disability affect progress in the curriculum: Due to Lucas's ADD, he struggles to attend to tasks and complete assignments. He has difficulty with organization and needs frequent redirection to prompt him to do his work. Academically, this has the most impact in ELA, where he is required to compose essays.

What types of accommodation, if any, are necessary for the student to make effective progress?

- Allow Lucas to sit in front of class.
- Provide note-taking support.
- Provide directions to assignments in a variety of ways (e.g., oral and written).
- Allow extra time on tests.
- Allow extra time on assignments.
- Encourage prewriting strategies.

Measurable Annual Goals

Current Performance Level: What can the student currently do? Lucas struggles to complete the majority of his work on time and to stay on task in class.

Work Completion: Lucas will remain on task with no more than two prompts per 30-minute period.

Communication with Teachers: Lucas will communicate with teachers appropriately regarding assignment completion 4 out of 5 days a week.

Writing: Lucas will be able to compose a topic sentence that reflects a main point, use three supporting details, and summarize with a conclusion in 3 out of 4 of his assignments. Lucas will create an organized essay by using prewriting strategies in 4 out of 5 assignments.

How will we know that the student has reached these goals? Teacher feedback, observation, work samples, progress reports, and report cards.

Service Delivery

What are the total service delivery needs of this student?

Focus on Measurable Annual Goals

Specialized Academic Instruction: 2X/week for 30 minutes (ex: educational specialist support)

Individual and Group Instruction: 2X/week for 30 minutes (ex: tutoring by academic coach or resource room)

Placement—Full Inclusion

IEP services are provided outside the general education classroom less than 21% of the time (80% inclusion).

Response Section

I certify that the goals in this IEP are those recommended by the team, and that the services included will be provided.

—Debbie Director,
Special Education Director
for Everytown School District, Everytown, USA

Individual IEP Participant Information—Classroom Observation Notes

Student: Lucas **Grade:** 9th
Class/location observed: English (Edith Educator)/30 min.
Observer: Ian Instructor, Special Education Teacher
Language: Age-appropriate

English Language Arts:

- Has difficulty proofreading and self-correcting work.
- Fails to develop ideas in writing, so written work is incomplete and too brief.

Social Studies:

- Has difficulty proofreading and self-correcting work.

- Fails to develop ideas in writing, so written work is incomplete and too brief.

Math: Age-appropriate
Science: Age-appropriate
Social-Emotional: Age-appropriate
Attention:

- Fails to pay attention to details or makes careless mistakes in schoolwork.
- Has difficulty organizing tasks and activities.
- Is easily distracted by outside influences.

9th-Grade Report for Lucas

Course Name	Grade	Teacher
Physical Science	B-	S. Smith
Algebra 1	B+	P. Phillip
World History	C	A. Allen
English Language Arts	D+	E. Educator

Special Education Director, Debbie Director

As special education director, it is your job to make sure the monies you have for special education are enough to provide for the educational needs of all students in the district. You think that Lucas is doing fine and would like to reduce his level of service.

You are the individual who convenes and runs the meeting. You also make the offer of FAPE during the meeting. Before you begin, set time limits for each section of the meeting, depending on how much time you have for this exercise. You'll want to say something like this to begin the meeting:

> Thank you for attending this annual IEP review meeting for Lucas. We are here to discuss Lucas's progress toward the goals listed in his IEP and whether any adjustments need to be made to the IEP as he progresses in 9th grade at Everytown High School. We will review Lucas's present levels of performance, strengths, and weaknesses, concerns of team members, progress toward his goals, proposed goals, and placement options. The IEP team will make decisions by consensus. Please be respectful of the views of others, actively participate by asking questions, and share your opinions. First, please introduce yourself and share your role in this meeting. [Allow the participants to introduce themselves.]

Next, you will lead the participants through a discussion of the agenda items. Invite the speakers to present during their respective sections of the agenda. Allow time for questions and comments by other IEP team members.

Parents

As Lucas's parent(s), you want to make sure your son receives the best education possible. You have been happy with Lucas's past services by Everytown School District, but you are concerned that he is struggling in his English Language Arts (ELA) class. You would like a higher level of support for Lucas both in this class and in world history. You have heard that there is an ELA class that is cotaught by a general education teacher and special education teacher. You think this might be a good fit. If not, you want more specialized instruction time.

You are also concerned that when you attended conferences last week, you noticed that Lucas sits in the back of the classroom in both ELA and Math. When you asked Lucas to show you his notes from ELA, they were very cryptic. You thought the IEP required note-taking support. Why isn't this happening?

General Education Teacher, Edith Educator

You teach Lucas's ELA course. You will discuss his overall grades and his strengths and weaknesses (as listed in the IEP). You'll admit that he sits in the back of your class and apologize for missing that accommodation. You also should note that while you asked a classmate to help Lucas with his notes, that student hasn't proven to be very reliable.

Really, you don't think Lucas needs this type of support, so you aren't very motivated to help him. This is especially true because he is very disruptive in your class because he frequently talks out of turn and walks around when he shouldn't. You think the special educator should do more to control Lucas's behavior in your class.

School Psychologist, Tara Therapist

You don't have any new testing to share about Lucas because this is only an annual IEP review. You just note that he was diagnosed with ADD 2 years ago, and has been receiving special education programs and services since then.

Everytown High School Principal, Manuel Manager

You don't have any specific information about Lucas's academic performance or his condition of ADD. What you do know is that he is a great kid who is an excellent citizen in your school community. You are there to support the team in coming up with a good plan for Lucas's success.

QUESTIONS FOR CONVERSATION (10 MINUTES)

Before the lesson, the facilitator will hand out the following questions to three different participants The facilitator can ask the selected participants to ask the questions during the Legal Lesson or devote a time after the Activity portion of the lesson for Q-and-A.

1. *When is it okay to not have a required member of the IEP team attend a meeting?* The IDEA regulations recognize that it can be hard to schedule IEP meetings, so they allow for some flexibility in participation. If the parent(s) and the district agree that a team member doesn't have to attend because the team does not plan to discuss that member's area of expertise, then that member's participation may be excused (IDEA, 20 U.S.C. § 1414[d][1][C]; 34 C.F.R. § 300.321[e]). Even if an IEP team member's area of expertise will be discussed, the member may still be excused from attending the meeting if both the LEA and parent(s) agree, and if that team member submits written input into the development of the IEP prior to the meeting. A parent's agreement to any such excusal must be in writing.

2. *What are transition services, and when do they need to be included in the IEP?* Transition services are intended to help a student with a disability move from school to postgraduation activities. Under IDEA, postschool activities include postsecondary education, vocational training, integrated employment, where individuals with disabilities work with many nondisabled peerscontinuing adult education, adult services, independent living, and participation in communities. The IEP should contain measurable postsecondary goals and a list of the transition services the district will provide to assist the student in meeting these goals. These must be included in a student's IEP in effect when the student turns 16, or earlier if determined appropriate by the IEP team (34 C.F.R. § 300.320[b]&[c] & 20 U.S.C. § 1414[d][1][A][i][VIII]). (See Lesson 7 for more information on this topic.)

3. *How do I handle the situation when the child's parents are divorced and only one attends the IEP meeting?* Divorce complicates the issue of IEP meetings. It is common for courts to specify the physical and legal custody or responsibility for the child when parents divorce. Under IDEA, both parents retain the right to participate in their child's IEP meetings unless state law or another legal document, such as a divorce decree, removes that right. For the purposes of the IEP meeting, it is the parent(s) with legal custody who retain(s) the right to engage in the decisionmaking process for the child's education. If only one parent has legal custody, then only that parent has the right to make educational decisions on behalf of the child; however, absent a court order to the contrary, both parents can still participate on the IEP team. If the court awards joint legal custody, then both parents are able to participate in the educational

decisionmaking at the IEP meeting. If parents with joint legal custody do not agree on the IEP, each one retains the right to file a due process claim to contest the IEP.

TEST YOUR KNOWLEDGE (5 MINUTES)

To review the information learned in this lesson, participants will play the Educational Benefit Game. Facilitators will discuss three placement scenarios in which participants will chose between two placement options to determine which placement is reasonably calculated to provide the student with a FAPE. The facilitator may pass out the scenarios or project them on a screen for participants to view.

Facilitator: Read the first scenario and possible placement and special education and related services offerings for a student with a disability.

Scenario 1. Rose, a teenager with ADHD who was found eligible as a child with an Other Heath Impairment, earned two Bs and three Fs during 9th grade. Her teachers reported overall good behavior at school, despite some inattention. Rose began seeing a counselor after her boyfriend, another student at the school, sexually assaulted her and her parents divorced. During her 10th grade year, Rose's grades were one A, three Bs, and two Ds. Her parents enrolled her in a private school mid-year due to her behavior of sneaking out at night and continuing to see her ex-boyfriend.

Placement 1	**Placement 2**
Public school with specially designed instruction to help her complete assignments and with counseling support from the school counselor.	Private school that offers individual and group psychotherapy to address matters such as her low self-esteem, her sexual "acting out," and her relationships with family members.

Facilitator: Ask to Participants: Please decide which placement option you believe is reasonably calculated to provide Rose with a FAPE.
Facilitator: Read the explanation of the outcome of the scenario to Participants

Scenario 1 is based on the case of Ashland Sch. Dist. v. Parents of R.J., 588 F.3d 1004 (9th Cir. 2009). In this case, the court ruled in favor of the public school placement because the private school did not provide special education and related services that were necessary for the student. The focus must be on the child's educational needs, and the special services provided by the private school placement were not necessary for these. Instead, the private placement was in response to the student's social or emotional problems.

Facilitator: Read the second scenario and possible placement and special education and related services offerings for a student with a disability.

Scenario 2. Tyler, a middle school student with a specific learning disability, has IEP goals that were essentially the same for three academic years. His academic test scores regressed significantly during this time period in all subjects. Tyler's placement was a combination of regular classroom and resource room setting, where he received support in English and mathematics. It is not clear whether Tyler was absent frequently or whether the school faithfully implemented his IEP.

Placement 1	**Placement 2**
Continue most of the time in the regular classroom. Increase the intensity of services by changing his setting from a combination general education/resource room setting to a small, structured class in an out of general education environment in all academic areas.	Move student to a private school placement where he can receive intensive academic support in each subject.

Facilitator: Ask to Participants: Please decide which placement option you believe is reasonably calculated to provide Tyler with a FAPE.
Facilitator: Read the explanation of the outcome of the scenario to Participants.

In Scenario 2, the intensification of support provided to the student in Placement 1 is the best for providing FAPE. It implements IDEA's mandate to place the student in the least restrictive environment (LRE). At this point, a private placement hasn't been shown to be necessary for FAPE (T.H. v. District of Columbia, 620 F. Supp. 2d 86 [D.C. 2009]).

Facilitator: Read the third scenario and possible placement and special education and related services offerings for a student with a disability.

Scenario 3. Kennedy, a high school student with Williams syndrome has an intellectual disability. She loves music, theater arts and choir and desires to take those classes. Kennedy had two negative experiences in choir and the school's choir director does not want her to participate anymore. She failed the class. Kennedy's test scores show high aptitude in the careers of child development, fashion, and childcare.

Placement 1

A public school placement focusing on living skills, functional academics, social skills, and vocational training in her areas of aptitude. The majority of the student's classes were in the general-education setting.

Placement 2

A private residential institution that focuses on functional living skills and music education, the area of the student's chosen career interest.

Facilitator: Ask to Participants: Please decide which placement option you believe is reasonably calculated to provide Kennedy with a FAPE.
Facilitator: Read the explanation of the outcome of the scenario to Participants.

In scenario 3, FAPE is provided by Placement 1. The student can make academic and social progress in the public school setting. Because the student lacks great aptitude in music, it is not necessary that the school provide this opportunity for her as part of her transition services. See *K.C. v. Mansfield Indep. Sch. Dist.*, 618 F. Supp. 2d (N.D. Tex. 2009).

ADDITIONAL RESOURCES

Klor, G. (2007). *Leading successful IEP teams: A guide to managing the people and the process.* Horsham, PA: LRP Publications.

Lake, S. E. (2010). *Slippery slope: The IEP missteps every team must know—and how to avoid them.* Horsham, PA: LRP Publications.

Pierangelo, R., & Guiliani, G. (2007). *Understanding, developing and writing effective IEPs.* Thousand Oaks, CA: Corwin.

U.S. Department of Education. *My child's special needs: A guide to the Individualized Education Program.* Retrieved from http://www2.ed.gov/parents/needs/speced/iepguide/index.html

Wright, P. W. D., & Wright, P. D. (2009). *Special education law* (2nd ed.). Hartfield, VA: Harbor House Law Press.

REFERENCES

Ashland Sch. Dist. v. Parents of R.J., 588 F.3d 1004 (9th Cir. 2009).

Bd. of Educ. of the Hendrick Hudson Central Sch. Dist. v. Rowley, 458 U.S. 176 (1982).

Individuals with Disabilities Education Act, 20 U.S.C. § 1414(d)(1)(A)(i)(IV). (2006).

K.C. v. Mansfield Indep. Sch. Dist., 618 F. Supp. 2d (N.D. Tex. 2009).

K.I. v. Montgomery Pub. Sch., 805 F. Supp. 2d 1283 (M.D. Ala. 2011).

Logsdon, A. (n.d.). Why parents file IDEA complaints, lawsuits: Conflicts causing parents to file formal complaints. About.com Learning Disabilities. Retrieved from http://learningdisabilities.about.com/od/disabilitylaws/tp/Reasons-for-Complaints.htm
New Milford Bd. of Educ. v. C.R, 431 F.App'x. 157 (3rd Cir. 2011).
Shuran, M. B., & Roblyer, M. D. (2012). Legal challenge: Characteristics of special education litigation in Tennessee schools. NASSP Bulletin, 96(1), 44–66.
Woods v. Northport Pub. Sch., 487 F.App'x. 968 (6th Cir. 2012).
Yell, M. L. (2016). The law and special education (4th ed.). Boston, MA: Pearson.
Zirkel, P. A., & Manchin, A. C. (2012). Special education case law "iceberg": An initial exploration of the underside. Journal of Law & Education, 41, 483–512.

What Does It Mean to Teach Students in the Least Restrictive Environment?

INTRODUCTION FOR FACILITATORS

The least restrictive environment, commonly known as LRE, is designed to include students with disabilities in general education settings with their nondisabled peers "to the maximum extent appropriate" (IDEA, 20 U.S.C. § 1412). The IEP team selects a student's placement from a continuum that includes instruction in general education classes, special classes, special schools, homebound instruction, and institutions or hospitals (IDEA, 34 C.F.R. § 300.115). The IEP team's goal is to select the most appropriate setting in which the child can receive a meaningful educational benefit from the program provided. The restrictiveness of a student's placement is measured by its proximity to the general education classroom on the continuum.

MATERIALS NEEDED

- LRE Law Scenarios Worksheets for each participant (see *Hook*);
- Facilitator script (see *Background, Purpose, and Objectives*);
- Continuum of Placements The Dating Game with a Twist Activity handouts for each Participant, and answer key (see *Activity*);
- Questions for Conversation on note cards (see *Questions for Conversation*); and
- Blank LRE Concept Maps for students to complete at the end of the lesson (see *Test Your Knowledge*).
- Optional: Objectives visually displayed (see *Background, Purpose, and Objectives*).

Before beginning the Hook portion of the lesson, the facilitator should pass out the LRE Concept Map that serves as the knowledge test for this lesson, and ask the participants to fill it out as they go through the lesson.

HOOK (15 MINUTES)

To begin the lesson, the facilitator will pass out the LRE Law Scenarios Worksheet to the participants and read the directions to them.

LRE Law Scenarios Worksheet

This activity gives you the opportunity to determine whether the student's placement and the local education agency's (LEA) actions in the scenarios are legal or illegal. In choosing a placement, the IEP team must consider several alternative placements, and select the one that is reasonably calculated to allow the student with a disability a meaningful educational benefit while educating the student with nondisabled peers to the maximum extent appropriate. LRE cannot be based on the following factors:

- Category of disability, severity of disability, or tradition;
- Disruption without evidence of behavior management attempts; or
- Cost for services, unless excessive (in most jurisdictions).

A student's placement must be based on an individual consideration of the student's educational needs.

Facilitators: Please take 5 minutes to review the scenarios shown in Table 5.1 and decide whether the placement is legal or illegal. After 5 minutes: Take the next 5 minutes to share with someone else your thoughts on the scenarios.

BACKGROUND, PURPOSE, AND OBJECTIVES OF THE LESSON (10 MINUTES)

Next, the facilitator will read the following **Facilitator Script,** or discuss the topics raised in the script in another way with the participants. It would be useful to display the objectives visually for them.

Facilitator Script

Facilitator: Today's legal lesson will cover the IDEA's least restrictive environment (LRE) requirement. Historically, students with disabilities were routinely excluded from the general education environment and were educated in isolated settings such as special education classrooms, private placements, and hospitals.

The Individuals with Disabilities Education Act (IDEA) requires that:

Table 5.1. LRE Scenarios

LRE Scenarios	Placement Legal?	Placement Illegal?
Scenario 1: T.J., a 4th-grader with autism, transfers to your school from an out-of-state school. The Special Education Director receives T.J.'s educational records, and identifies that T.J.'s last school provided him with 20 hours of Applied Behavior Analysis (ABA). ABA is expensive, and no one is trained in ABA at your school. The Director tells T.J.'s mom, "T.J. will be placed in our autism classroom with other children with autism." T.J.'s mom says she would like T.J.'s ABA to continue. The Director says, "Sorry, that's not something that our district provides. Plus, his file states that he has behavior issues, so he is best off in our autism room."		
Scenario 2: K.P. is an elementary school student with ADHD and learning disabilities in reading and math. In her annual IEP meeting, the IEP team reviewed K.P.'s new psychological report and considered whether she should attend regular classes full-time with supplementary aides and services and whether K.P. should spend less than 20% of her school week in a separate special education class. The team decided that K.P. would be best served by attending regular classes and spending 25% of her time receiving services in a separate class. Her parents are upset by this placement. Although they didn't mention it during the meeting, they claim that K.P.'s LRE is in a special day school that offers multisensory instruction.		
Scenario 3: Thomas is a student with dyslexia, ADHD, and depressive mood disorder. He has been educated in a Teaching Approach to Mastery (TAM) classroom with both regular and special education students, supported by accommodations and assistance, for the past 3 years. Although initially he was making progress in the curriculum, his progress has slowed. The school psychologist's report shows severe discrepancies between his ability and his achievement in reading and mathematics. The Special Education Director says, "We are proud of the fact that Thomas is being educated with his nondisabled peers. He should remain in his current placement as the least restrictive environment."		
Scenario 4: In Sally's IEP meeting, her parents insist that she needs to attend a private day school in order to receive an educational benefit. The LEA's Special Education Director disagrees, saying, "Sally can receive an educational benefit through the services that are offered within the LEA, so the LEA is the least restrictive environment." In order to resolve this disagreement, the superintendent recommends that the parties split the difference: the LEA will pay the parents $19,000 this academic year so that Sally is able to attend the private school, and the parents agree that Sally will return to the public school next year to receive her education.		

Table 5.1. LRE Scenarios, Continued

LRE Scenarios	Placement Legal?	Placement Illegal?
Scenario 5: Manuel is in 3rd grade and receives 27.5 hours per week of special education. His writing instruction consists of 3 hours per week in the regular classroom. Manuel's regular classroom teacher announced she was taking leave for at least a month, so Manuel's IEP team convened to determine how to handle his education in her absence. School-based team members recommended he have writing instruction in the resource room (RR), but his mother objected. The Special Education Director moved Manuel's writing instruction to the RR during his teacher's absence without modifying his IEP. When the teacher returned, Manuel continued in the RR for writing. His parents claim that failure to immediately return him to his original placement when his teacher returned violates LRE.		

Figure 5.1. Continuum of Placements

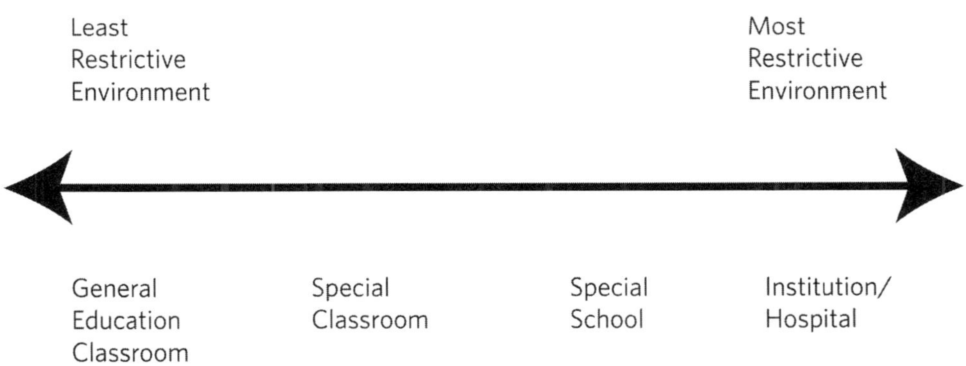

> To the maximum extent appropriate, children with disabilities . . . are educated with children who are not disabled, and that special classes, separate schooling, or other removal of children with disabilities from the general educational environment occurs only when the nature or severity of the disability is such that education in general education classes with the use of supplementary aids and services cannot be achieved satisfactorily. (20 U.S.C. § 1412[a][5])

The goal of this provision is to give students with disabilities access to the curriculum that is being taught to their nondisabled peers, and to help them learn age-appropriate skills. The general education environment is presumed to be the least restrictive setting because it is the location where nondisabled students are educated. However, the general education environment is not the right setting for every child. When determining FAPE and LRE for a student with a disability, that student's IEP team must consider a continuum of potential services and placements to determine which is best suited to meet that child's unique needs (see Figure 5.1).

Table 5.1. LRE Scenarios: Answer Key

LRE Scenarios Answer Key	Placement Legal?	Placement Illegal?
Scenario 1 Summary: T.J., a 4th-grader with autism, is placed by the Special Education Director in the autism classroom with other children with autism, in part due to behavior problems, and is also not provided with ABA services, over his mother's objections. *Rationale*: The IEP team, not the Director of Special Education, determines placement. Category of disability cannot be a factor in determining placement, and neither can cost of services in many jurisdictions. Also, disruption without evidence of behavior management attempts cannot be used as a reason to provide a more restrictive placement.		X
Scenario 2 Summary: The IEP team for K.P., an elementary school student with ADHD and learning disabilities in reading and math, decides to place her in a regular class, spending 25% of her time receiving services in a separate class. Her parents want her in a special day school that offers multisensory instruction. *Rationale:* The IEP team considered several alternative placements based on the new report and determined the appropriate placement for K.P. The parents did not mention their desire for the multisensory placement during the meeting. Because the LEA was able to show that K.P. could receive a satisfactory education by spending 75% of her time in regular classes and 25% in special classes, a day school was not her LRE (*Porter v. Illinois State Bd. of Educ.*, 2014).	X	
Scenario 3 Summary: Thomas, a student with dyslexia, ADHD, and depressive mood disorder, has slow academic progress in a TAM classroom. The LEA thinks he should stay in this placement. *Rationale:* Because Thomas is not succeeding academically despite supplementary aides and services, his instruction and placement in the inclusive setting is not reasonably calculated to provide him with an educational benefit. The least restrictive environment must be a setting where the child makes appropriate progress. In this case, continuing his placement in the TAM classroom violates the school's responsibility to provide a free appropriate public education to Thomas (*Fisher v. Bd. of Educ. of Christina Sch. Dist.*, 2003).		X
Scenario 4 Summary: Sally's parents want her to attend a private day school, but the LEA wants to educate her itself. The superintendent makes a deal for her to spend 1 year in the private school and then return to the LEA. *Rationale:* The parties cannot enter into an agreement to determine Sally's placement for the subsequent school year regardless of her educational needs. (*New Fairfield BOE v. Cortese*, 2005).		X

Table 5.1. LRE Scenarios: Answer Key, Continued

LRE Scenarios Answer Key	Place-ment Legal?	Place-ment Illegal?
Scenario 5 Summary: Manuel's 3rd-grade teacher takes leave for a month. His IEP team changes his writing placement to the RR while she is gone and doesn't return him to the classroom when the teacher returns. *Rationale:* Manuel's change in placement during the time when his teacher was on leave was only a minor, nonactionable violation of his IEP, because he was receiving writing instruction and making progress in the resource room setting. However, by not returning Manuel to his regular education classroom placement for writing when his teacher returned, the LEA denied him free appropriate public education because he had behavioral goals he needed to meet in the regular education environment. The court provided him with compensatory education so he could pursue the behavioral goals in his IEP (*Madeline P. v. Anchorage Sch. Dist.*, 2009).	X	X

Placements, as with all IEP decisions, must be determined on a case-by-case basis. LEAs may be failing to offer students LRE when they move a student out of the general education classroom based solely on his or her categories of disability or areas of learning deficits without first attempting to support the student's learning in the general education environment (Lake, 2010). LEAs also violate LRE when they place a student in a particular learning environment based only on a school's available programs and services, or solely on cost factors, rather than tailoring the IEP and services to meet the individual needs of each child (Lake, 2010).

The following two cases illustrate districts' failures to consider less restrictive alternatives for students. In the first case, the IEP team for a student with Attention Deficit Hyperactivity Disorder (ADHD) who experienced behavior and academic difficulties at his middle school recommended that he be placed in a specialized high school for students with disabilities. Instead of accepting this placement, his parents enrolled him in a private school and filed a due process challenge. In the private school, students with disabilities spent lunch, gym, and homeroom with general education students, and had their academic courses taught separately by the same teachers as the general education students.

Reviewing this decision, the court held that the LEA violated the LRE requirement by not mainstreaming the student to the maximum extent appropriate for his individual needs because the student's behavior problems in middle school had lessened after the district provided an aide for him; this fact was not considered by the IEP team when they recommended the specialized high school. The specialized high school placement also would not have allowed the student to interact with his general education peers (*Jennifer D.*

v. New York City Dept. of Educ., 2008). In the second case, an LEA initially placed a student with autism into an integrated preschool program where she was able to learn while she interacted with nondisabled peers. Although the student made academic and social progress in that environment, the LEA recommended placement in a self-contained classroom for the subsequent year. The child's parents disagreed and placed her in an integrated private preschool program with a 1:1 aide. The court found that the LEA had not satisfied the LRE requirement because it had not considered accommodations (such as an aide) that would allow the student to continue in the integrated classroom rather than a self-contained classroom where she would only learn with other students with disabilities (*G.B. v. Tuxedo Union Free Sch. Dist.*, 2010). To make placement decisions, LEAs need to consider:

> [T]he nature and severity of the student's disability, the student's specialized educational needs, the link between those needs . . . and the services offered, and the extent to which the placement represents the least restrictive environment (*Branham v. District of Columbia*, 2005, p. 12).

The specific objectives for today's lesson are for you to be able to:

1. Better understand LRE;
2. Describe the continuum of alternative placements;
3. Identify factors that schools can and cannot use to determine the student placement standard; and
4. Evaluate whether student placements comply with LRE requirements.

ACTIVITY (30 MINUTES)

Continuum of Placements—The Dating Game with a Twist

The facilitator will organize the participants into five groups:

- General education classroom,
- Special classes,
- Special schools,
- Hospital/institution/homebound, and
- Potential students.

Each group will be given a brief description of three potential students. The activity is broken down into three parts:

1. During the first 10 minutes, the participants review the materials and prepare for the activity.

2. During the second 10 minutes, the participants provide the student overviews and the placement pitches.
3. During the remaining 10 minutes, the facilitator explains the court's decisions on the cases, and invites class discussion about the outcomes.

Facilitator: An IEP team must place a student with a disability in the LRE. To do this, they must consider a continuum of placements, and not automatically opt for placement in the general education classroom if that is not most appropriate. On one end of the continuum, educating a child in the general education classroom is the initial preference, and should be the placement unless the child cannot satisfactorily receive an educational benefit from the education provided there, even with the use of supplementary services (*J.H. v. Fort Bend Indep. Sch. Dist.*, 2012). At the other, most restrictive end of the continuum, schools are responsible for paying for the child to be placed in a residential treatment facility in order to make meaningful educational progress, such as an institution or hospital (*M.H. v. Monroe-Wodbury Cent. Sch. Dist.*, 2008).

IEP teams should consider placement in the general education classroom first and then, if that does not meet the student's individual needs, move down the continuum to consider more restrictive alternatives. Bear in mind that the ultimate LRE may be an environment that is actually more restrictive in structure than the general education classroom, depending on the *individual* needs of the student.

Please use the next 10 minutes to discuss the three scenarios and consider each student's educational needs in light of their potential placements. If you are in the "potential students" group, think about which of the two alternatives would be the most likely setting in which the student could receive a meaningful educational benefit. If you are in a placement group, only consider the student profiles where your placement is listed as a possibility, and determine if you can offer the student a meaningful educational benefit in your group's assigned setting.

After the first 10 minutes, the potential student group will provide a 1-minute overview of each student's needs, one at a time (this may be done by reading the scenario aloud). After each student overview, the two relevant placement groups will each respond with a 1-minute pitch (planned during the initial 10 minutes) on why their placement is or is not the appropriate setting for the student. We will begin with the pitch from the least restrictive setting.

Handout for Continuum of Placements—The Dating Game with a Twist Activity

Student 1, Jake (general education classroom vs. special classes). Jake, a 14-year-old child with an IQ of 48, has significant cognitive delays. His academic achievement scores range from the kindergarten to 2nd-grade level. During 6th grade, Jake attended general education classes. In two of those classes, science and social studies, he was provided a full-time aide, and his teachers modified all of his assignments to accommodate his skill level. His teachers noted that he did not pay attention in class and would not comply with simple directions.

As the year progressed, he began to act out by shutting down and refusing to do any work in these classes. His behavior was not disruptive to the other students in the class. Because he was taught primarily by teaching aides and tutors, he had limited interaction with the other students in his classes. He received failing grades in his science and social studies classes for most of the year, but his final grades were recorded as Bs.

Student 2, Kyle (special education classroom vs. special school). Kyle, a preschool student with a hearing impairment, has been receiving educational services at a local private hearing and speech center. The IEP team recommends that Kyle be placed in the special education classroom for 6 hours a day, 3 days per week. He and his teacher would use an FM auditory trainer system to communicate. He would also receive 30 minutes per week of classroom assistance from a deaf educator, and 30 minutes a day of speech and language therapy when at school. Kyle's parents refused to sign the IEP and continued his education at the private hearing and speech center. They allege that the school's special education room is not conducive to learning by a student with a hearing impairment. The room is large, with high ceilings and no carpeting, so it is not acoustically correct. In addition, the heating and cooling systems are very noisy. Moreover, the special education teacher is not trained in working with students with hearing impairments.

Student 3, Mildred (special school vs. hospitalization or institutionalization). Mildred, a teenager with emotional and educational disabilities, has been enrolled in a private day school where she receives educational and counseling services. She is earning Cs in all of her classes, and her therapist reports that she is making progress socially and emotionally. Her parents have asked for a change of Mildred's placement to the residential treatment portion of this school because they are concerned about her mental stability. Although she is making progress in the day program, they are concerned that her progress could easily be reversed if her painful memories resurface.

Answer Key for Continuum of Placements Activity

Student 1, Jake. The school district changed Jake's IEP to move him into special education classes rather than the general education classes for science and social studies. He remained in general education classes for his other subjects. This move was upheld by the court because Jake was not receiving an educational benefit in the general education classes. His lack of benefit was evidenced by his inability to access the general education curriculum (even with adaptations and modifications) and his frustrated and noncompliant behaviors in the classes (*J.H. v. Fort Bend Indep. Sch. Dist.*, 2012).

Student 2, Kyle. The LRE placement for Kyle is the private hearing and speech center. The special education class placement was not appropriate because of the acoustical difficulties in the room and the lack of appropriate training of the primary special education teacher. The IEP did not address the parents' concerns in a manner that would allow Kyle to receive an educational benefit from the special education classroom. It only suggested that the heating and cooling system be turned off while Kyle attended school, but did not explain how the climate would be controlled in the room during this time (*Wilson Cnty. Sch. Sys. v. Clifton*, 2000).

Student 3, Mildred. Because Mildred is making satisfactory educational progress, as evidenced by her passing grades, the special day school placement meets LRE requirements. Although the parents' concerns about her mental stability are valid, a court will not require a school district to change a student's placement based on a potential problem that has not yet materialized (*M.H. v. Monroe-Woodbury Cent. Sch. Dist.*, 2008).

QUESTIONS FOR CONVERSATION (10 MINUTES)

Before the lesson, the facilitator will hand out the following questions to three different participants. The facilitator can ask the selected participants to ask the questions during the lesson or may devote a time after the Activity portion of the lesson for Q-and-A.

1. What rights do parents/guardians have if they disagree with the placement the other members of the IEP team recommend? Parents/guardians have several options if they disagree with the recommended placement. First, parents/guardians should ask for the placement they believe is appropriate during the IEP team meeting. Second, they can formally note their disagreement by signing the IEP form and indicating that they do not agree with the IEP for their child. If either of these things happens in most jurisdictions, the school will implement the IEP as written, and the LEA is not required to take any further action to resolve the disagreement. However, in the 9th Circuit, which includes Alaska, Arizona, California, Idaho, Montana, Nevada, Oregon, and Washington, an IEP cannot be implemented over a parent/guardian's objection.

Parents/guardians' third option is filing a due process complaint to contest the IEP's placement as inappropriate. In this scenario, the LEA should implement the placement specified in the IEP unless the "Stay Put" provision of the IDEA applies, such as it does in the 9th Circuit.

Stay Put. The IDEA's Stay Put provision is relevant when an IEP team is recommending a change of placement and a due process complaint is pending; it requires that the student remain in the current educational placement unless the LEA and parents agree to a different placement (20 U.S.C. § 1415[j]). If

Figure 5.2. LRE Concept Map

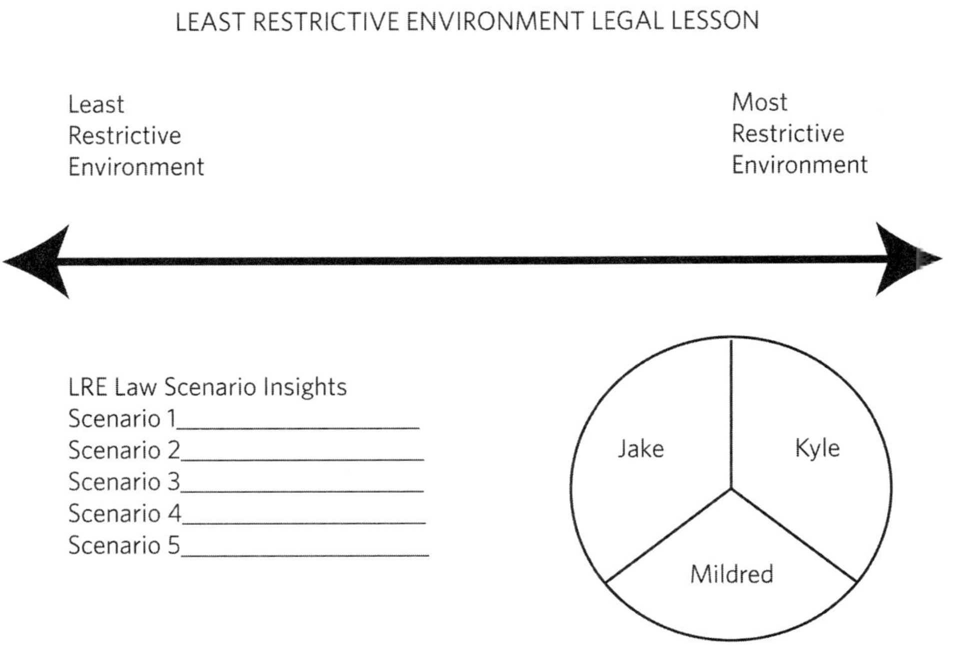

the due process complaint is successful, the parents/guardians can have their child placed in the educational environment the hearing officer deems appropriate for their child.

Private Placement. Finally, if the parents/guardians believe that a private school placement is the LRE for their child instead of the placement included in the IEP, they may inform the school of their disagreement and enroll their child in the private school at their own expense. If the parents file a due process complaint and are successful, the hearing officer can require the LEA to reimburse the parents for the tuition expenses because the IEP's placement was inappropriate (34 C.F.R. § 300.148).

2. Can the LRE for a given student change from year to year? Yes. IDEA requires an annual review of each student's IEP, more often if appropriate. During this meeting, the IEP team reviews the student's progress toward IEP goals. If the student is not meeting those goals, the team should consider additional supports for the student, including an alternative placement that may be in a more restrictive environment. If the student is exceeding IEP goals, the team should consider whether the child is likely to receive a meaningful educational benefit in a less restrictive environment.

3. How should the IEP team consider the effect on the education of other students when a student with a disability is educated in a general education classroom? Courts across the country use different legal tests to determine whether LEAs have complied with the LRE requirement (*Daniel R. R. v. State Bd. of Educ.*, 1989; *Hartmann v.*

Loudoun Cnty. Bd. of Educ., 1997; *Roncker v. Walter*, 1983; *Sacramento City Unified Sch. Dist. v. Rachel H.*, 1994). These legal frameworks guide school officials when they make placement decisions, as they consider the effect of a disabled student's presence on the learning of classmates. One way to ask this question is whether the student's behavior is either disruptive or requires an inordinate amount of attention from the teacher (Hartmann, 1997; *Sacramento City Unified Sch. Dist. v. Rachel H.*, 1994).

TEST YOUR KNOWLEDGE (5 MINUTES)

The facilitator will pass out the LRE Concept Map (see Figure 5.2) at the beginning of the session. Each student will complete a concept map on the topics addressed during the session. At this point in the lesson, the facilitator should provide the participants with 5 minutes to complete their concept maps.

ADDITIONAL RESOURCES

Colker, R., & Waterson, J. K. (2011). *Special education advocacy.* Providence, NJ: LexisNexis.

Hulett, K. E. (2009). *Legal aspects of special education.* Upper Saddle River, NJ: Pearson.

REFERENCES

Branham v. District of Columbia, 427 F.3d 7 (D.C. Cir. 2005).
Daniel R. R. v. State Bd. of Educ., 874 F.2d 1036 (5th Cir. 1989).
Fisher v. Bd. of Educ. of Christina Sch. Dist., 856 A.2d 552 (Del. 2003).
G.B. v. Tuxedo Union Free Sch. Dist., 751 F.Supp.2d 552 (S.D. N.Y. 2010).
Hartmann v. Loudoun Cnty. Bd. of Educ., 118 F.3d 996 (4th Cir. 1997).
Individuals with Disabilities Education Act, 20 U.S.C. §§ 1412; 1415(j) (2004).
J.H. v. Fort Bend Indep. Sch. Dist., 482 F.App'x. 915 (5th Cir. 2012).
Jennifer D. v. New York City Dept. of Educ., 550 F.Supp.2d 420 (S.D. N.Y. 2008).
Lake, S. E. (2010). *Slippery slope! The IEP missteps every team must know and how to avoid them.* Horsham, PA: LRP Publications.
Madeline P. v. Anchorage Sch. Dist., 265 P.3d 308 (Alaska 2009).
M.H. v. Monroe-Wodbury Cent. Sch. Dist., 296 F.App'x. 126 (2nd Cir. 2008).
New Fairfield BOE v. Cortese, 2005 WL 647556, No. CV030349701S (Sup. Ct. CT. Jan. 24, 2005).
Porter v. Illinois State Bd. of Educ., 6 N.E.3d 424 (Ill. Ct. App. 2014).
Roncker v. Walter, 700 F.2d 1058 (6th Cir. 1983).
Sacramento City Unified Sch. Dist. v. Rachel H., 14 F.3d 1398 (9th Cir. 1994).
Wilson Cnty. Sch. Sys. v. Clifton, 41 S.W.3d 645 (Tenn. Ct. App. 2000). 34 C.F.R. § 300.403 (2000).

How Are Students with Disabilities Disciplined Differently?

INTRODUCTION FOR FACILITATORS

Student discipline is one of the most common causes of special education lawsuits (Katsiyannis, Losinski, & Prince, 2012). In many instances, courts have found that school districts violated the law by failing to follow required procedures when disciplining students with disabilities. For example, a district removed a student with autism from his school for kicking the principal in the knee. The district reasoned that because the student inflicted serious bodily injury, it could remove the student without first conducting a Manifestation Determination—the meeting that is required under the Individuals with Disabilities Education Act (IDEA), where the Individualized Education Program (IEP) team reviews whether a student's misbehavior was a manifestation of the student's disability. The student's parents, however, successfully argued that the discipline was illegal because the principal's sharp knee pain did not fit within the IDEA's definition of serious bodily injury (*Bisbee Unified Sch. Dist.*, 2010).

In another case, a court held that a student was denied a Free Appropriate Public Education (FAPE) because the student's behavior was impeding her learning, but the school had not implemented a Behavioral Intervention Plan (BIP)— a document addressing how employees should respond and prevent undesired student behavior (*Metro. Bd. of Pub. Educ. v. Bellamy*, 2004). Finally, another court found that the school district erred when it failed to provide a Manifestation Determination before disciplining a 3rd-grader. Although the student did not have an IEP, the court reasoned that school officials had sufficient reason to suspect the student had a disability when they referred him to an outside mental health agency (*Jackson v. Northwest Local Sch.l Dist.*, 2010).

In addition to litigation, school districts are under heightened scrutiny because many groups, including the U.S. Department of Education, Congress, state legislatures, and advocacy organizations, have become increasingly interested in protecting students with disabilities from improper discipline techniques and procedures in schools (Butler, 2012; Fantz, 2008; Keeping All Students Safe Act, 2013; TASH, 2011). In 2009, the U.S. Government

Accountability Office (GAO) presented testimony to Congress regarding the use of restraints and seclusion in schools. The report detailed hundreds of alleged instances of improper discipline resulting in abuse or death of students with disabilities (U.S. GAO, 2009, pp. 5–8). For example, the report describes an allegation where 5-year-old students with muscular difficulties sustained injuries such as broken arms from a special education teacher who allegedly used bungee cords and duct tape to restrain them (U.S. GAO, 2009, p. 6). In another case, the parents of a 13-year-old Georgia boy with Attention Deficit Hyperactivity Disorder (ADHD) brought suit after their son committed suicide as he was held involuntarily in a seclusion room as a form of punishment (*King v. Pioneer Reg'l Educ. Serv. Agency*, 2009). In 2012, the parents of a student with autism sued a Florida district for restraining their son 89 times in a 14-month period (*J.P.M. v. Palm Beach County Sch. Bd.*, 2013).

In light of the intensified attention to the discipline of students with disabilities, it is vital to train all school employees about the law surrounding this issue. Therefore, Lesson 6 provides guidance on how to prevent improper disciplinary actions such as illegal suspensions and expulsions. Key terms found in the relevant legislation, including Manifestation Determination, Positive Behavioral Interventions and Supports (PBIS), Functional Behavior Assessments (FBAs), Behavior Intervention Plans (BIPs), and Interim Alternative Education Setting (IAES), are defined below. Participants will also learn how to apply the law to common discipline scenarios.

MATERIALS NEEDED

The facilitator(s) should organize the following items prior to the lesson:

- Discipline Scenarios for each participant (see *Hook* and *Activity*);
- Facilitator script (see Background, Purpose, and Objectives);
- Definition Cards for each small group, and answer key (see *Activity*);
- Questions typed/written on three handouts (see *Questions for Conversation*);
- Six Legal Violations Skit scripts (see *Test Your Knowledge*);
- Index cards for each participant (see *Test Your Knowledge*); and
- Optional: Objectives visually displayed (see *Background, Purpose, and Objectives*).

HOOK (10-15 MINUTES)

To begin the lesson, the facilitator will hand out the Discipline Scenarios appearing in Table 6.1. The participants will individually read each scenario and check the box that corresponds with their best guess as to whether the discipline was legal or illegal. The facilitator should explain that this initial

Table 6.1. Discipline Scenarios

	Legal?	Illegal?
Andrew, a 9th-grader who is hearing-impaired and receiving special education services, accidentally left a pocket knife in his backpack after camping last weekend. After discovering the knife in a locker search, the principal told Andrew that, due to the school's zero-tolerance weapons policy, he was expelled for the remaining 3 months of the academic year, and would need to stay home starting tomorrow. Was the expulsion legal?		
Legal Support for Your Conclusion:		
Santiago is a freshman in high school and does not receive special education and related services. After a classmate teased him in the cafeteria, Santiago punched him in the face, causing a minor injury. The school suspended Santiago for 14 days. During his suspension, his parents informed the school that Santiago had an IEP at his former middle school. They explained that he has an emotional disturbance and his lack of impulse control causes him to become violent. At the beginning of the year, Santiago's parents wrote a note to his teacher about his previous IEP and disability, but the teacher did not pass the information along to the special education director. Was the suspension legal?		
Legal Support for Your Conclusion:		
Mona is a 6th-grade student with autism who has an IEP. After a boy came too close to her, she pushed him down the stairs. Luckily, no one was injured. The principal believes that Mona should be removed from the school because she is jeopardizing the safety of the other students. Mona's IEP team had a Manifestation Determination meeting and decided that her misbehavior had a direct and substantial relationship to her diagnosis of autism. The IEP team determined that Mona's misbehavior was a result of her IEP not being properly implemented. Therefore, the IEP team decided that no punishment was warranted for Mona, but made plans for a Functional Behavioral Assessment (FBA) to occur, which will result in the creation of a Behavior Intervention Plan (BIP). Were the IEP team's actions legal?		
Legal Support for Your Conclusion:		
Isaac is a student with a traumatic brain injury (TBI) who is receiving special education services. The school has suspended him for 8 days for fighting during this academic year. Today he got into another fight and was suspended for 3 days. When Isaac's parents came to school to pick him up, they asked when his IEP team will meet to discuss his discipline. The principal explained that there is no reason for the IEP team to meet because the administrators make the discipline decisions. Were the principal's actions legal?		
Legal Support for Your Conclusion:		

Table 6.1. Discipline Scenarios, Continued

	Legal?	Illegal?
Zhong is a 7th-grade boy who has a specific learning disability and receives special education services. He has already been suspended for a total of 8 days this academic year for hitting teachers. Today he kicked a teacher, but did not cause a serious injury. The principal recommends that Zhong be suspended for 3 days. Zhong's IEP team held a Manifestation Determination and decided that his misbehavior did not have a direct and substantial relationship to his specific learning disability. The IEP team determined that Zhong's misbehavior was not the result of improper implementation of his IEP. Therefore, the IEP Team decided that Zhong's 3-day suspension was warranted, determining that a home placement was appropriate. Zhong's school arranged for him to receive assignments at home to ensure his continued progress toward his IEP goals. All of his special education services will also continue while he is at home. The IEP team also made plans for a Functional Behavioral Assessment (FBA) to occur that will result in the creation of a Behavior Intervention Plan (BIP). Were the school's actions legal?		
Legal Support for Your Conclusion:		

activity is a pretest to help the participants begin thinking about the legal issues. They should not attempt to complete the portions of the table that ask for legal support. They will discuss the legal support for each conclusion in the activity section of this lesson.

BACKGROUND, PURPOSE, AND OBJECTIVES OF THE LESSON (5 MINUTES)

Next, the facilitator will read the following **Facilitator Script** to the participants or paraphrase the information (if there is more than one facilitator, you may choose to split the script among them). The facilitator may consider having the Objectives displayed visually so that the participants can refer to them during the lesson.

Facilitator Script

Facilitator: Today's legal lesson will cover what procedures we must follow when disciplining students with disabilities. Why do you believe the law requires us to follow special procedures?

The facilitator fields responses from the participants and then responds: Students with disabilities have traditionally been expelled and suspended from schools more often than their peers. In fact, even though special legal protections exist, students with disabilities continue to be suspended and expelled more often than other students (Williams, Pazey, Shelby, & Yates, 2013).

Student discipline is one of the most common causes of special education lawsuits (Katsiyannis et al., 2012).

It is important you recognize that school employees *can* discipline students with disabilities, but must carefully follow the legal parameters defined by court cases, the IDEA, and Section 504. The U.S. Supreme Court decided that students with disabilities are entitled to a higher level of due process than general education students (*Honig v. Doe*, 1988). As a result, the IDEA has detailed the type of due process that school districts must provide to students receiving special education services. Also, in order to comply with Section 504, the federal civil rights law prohibiting disability discrimination, districts must not impose discipline on students with disabilities in a discriminatory manner. For example, districts could not have discipline procedures for students with disabilities that are harsher than procedures for nondisabled students. We will focus only on the federal law; however, be aware that states can modify the discipline procedures surrounding students with disabilities, as long as they adhere to the federal requirements.

The specific objectives for today's lesson are for you to:

1. Define Manifestation Determination procedures, including the 10-Day Rule,
2. Describe Positive Behavioral Interventions and Supports (PBIS),
3. Distinguish Functional Behavior Assessments (FBAs) from Behavior Intervention Plans (BIPs), and
4. Identify when it is legal to remove a student with a disability to an Interim Alternative Education Setting (IAES).

Please feel free to ask any questions throughout or at the end of the lesson.

ACTIVITY (20–25 MINUTES)

The facilitator will divide the participants into groups of six. Each group member will be given one of the Definition Cards found in Figure 6.1 (if the groups are smaller than six, then the facilitator will need to give some group members more than one card). The facilitator will instruct the participants to serve as the expert on the topic of their assigned card. First, each participant should review his or her card. When everyone has had an opportunity to review the cards, the small groups will return to each scenario from the "Discipline Scenarios" table and discuss as a group whether the discipline was legal or illegal. They should use the Definition Cards to provide the legal rationale to support their conclusions.

Figure 6.1. Definition Cards

MANIFESTATION DETERMINATION

A student with a disability should be disciplined in a manner similar to students without disabilities unless there is a connection between his or her disability and his or her misconduct. IDEA stipulates that a Manifestation Determination must occur before a student with a disability may be suspended for a total of *more than* 10 days during a school year. A Manifestation Determination is a meeting conducted by the parents/guardians and members of the child's IEP team (as determined by the parents/guardians and the LEA). Often, this group is simply referred to as the IEP team. When a student with a disability is suspended for 10 *or fewer* days during a school year, no Manifestation Determination is needed.

At the Manifestation Determination, the IEP team reviews all relevant material to decide whether a student's misbehavior was

1. caused by, or had a direct and substantial relationship to, the student's disability; or
2. a direct result of the school's failure to properly implement the student's IEP.

In other words, if the IEP team determines that the student's misbehavior is related to or caused by the student's disability, the student *cannot* be suspended for more than 10 days. However, if the IEP team determines that the student's misbehavior is *not* related to or caused by the student's disability, the student *can* be suspended for more than 10 days.

When a student with a disability is suspended for more than 10 days, the school *must* continue to provide special education and related services outlined in student's IEP. Also, IDEA's 2006 regulations specify that school employees may consider unique circumstances on a case-by-case basis when determining whether a change of placement is appropriate for a student with a disability who violates school conduct rules (34 C.F.R. § 300.530[a]).

EMERGENCY EXCEPTIONS FOR IMMEDIATE REMOVAL

A significant exception exists when suspending students with disabilities. A Manifestation Determination does not need to occur before a student is removed from a school setting if the student was "at school, on school premises, or at a school function" (34 CFR § 300.530[g][1]-[3]), and the student:

1. caused serious bodily injury,
2. possessed a weapon,
3. knowingly possessed or used illegal drugs, or
4. sold or solicited a controlled substance (34 C.F.R. § 300.530[g]).

Even if one of these four emergency exceptions has occurred, a Manifestation Determination must still occur within 10 days of the student's removal. Therefore, in nonemergency situations, a Manifestation Determination must happen *before* the student is removed from the current education program for more than 10 days. However, if any of the four emergency situations has occurred, the student can be removed immediately, but a Manifestation Determination still must occur within 10 days.

If one of the above exceptions has not occurred, but a school administrator believes that a student is a danger to self or others, the school official can request (*cont.*)

EMERGENCY EXCEPTIONS FOR IMMEDIATE REMOVAL, CONTINUED

that an impartial hearing officer remove the student to an alternative setting. The school official usually needs to show that keeping the student in the current placement is substantially likely to result in injury to the student or others.

10-DAY RULE

Suspending students with disabilities for more than 10 days is considered a change of placement under IDEA. The 10-Day Rule requires that before a student with a disability is removed from a placement for more than 10 school days within a school year, the IEP team must conduct a Manifestation Determination within 10 school days of the decision to remove the student.

If one of the four emergency exceptions has occurred (e.g., student has caused serious bodily injury), then a student *can* be removed before a Manifestation Determination has taken place as long as the Manifestation Determination takes place within 10 days of the suspension. The 10 days of removal may be consecutive or nonconsecutive; however, if nonconsecutive, they must constitute a pattern of exclusion. To determine whether a series of brief suspensions constitute a pattern of exclusion and require a Manifestation Determination, consider:

1. Whether the series of removals totals more than 10 school days in an academic year.
2. Whether the student's behavior is substantially similar to the student's behavior in prior incidents that resulted in the series of removals.
3. Whether there are additional factors indicating a pattern of removal, such as the length of each removal, the total amount of time the child has been removed, and the proximity of the removals to one another (34 C.F.R. § 300.536).

Overall, it is crucial to analyze whether the student has been removed from school for more than 10 days. Therefore, if a student was suspended for 3 days in April and then 9 days in May, the student would be removed for a total of 12 days. If these two brief suspensions constitute a removal from placement, the IEP team must convene for a Manifestation Determination to decide whether the student's misbehavior was 1) a result of, or substantially related to, the student's disability, or 2) a direct result of failing to implement the student's IEP. Also, a Manifestation Determination does not need to occur when students with disabilities are removed from their placements for 10 days or less.

POSITIVE BEHAVIORAL INTERVENTIONS AND SUPPORTS (PBIS)

According to IDEA, the IEP team must consider using Positive Behavioral Interventions and Supports (PBIS) for any student whose behavior impedes his or her learning or the learning of others (20 U.S.C. § 1414(d)(3)(B)(i)). IDEA states that the education of children with disabilities "can be made more effective by . . . providing incentives for whole-school approaches, scientifically based early reading programs, positive behavioral interventions and supports, and early intervening services" (20 U.S.C. § 1401[c][5][F]).

Two examples of PBIS include Functional Behavioral Assessments (FBAs) and Behavior Intervention Plans (BIPs). A professional trained in behavior intervention conducts a FBA to determine the underlying causes of a student's problem behavior. For example, a FBA could analyze whether a student is kicking to escape a challenging activity or to gain attention from others. A BIP is then developed to prevent problematic behaviors and increase appropriate behaviors. For example, if a student was kicking a desk to gain attention from others, the BIP may instruct the school employees to ignore the kicking behavior and teach replacement behaviors that the student could engage in to gain attention.

According to the commentary of the 2006 IDEA Regulations, an IEP must address a behavior if the student has a history of a problem behavior or if it can be anticipated that the student will engage in the behavior (34 C.F.R. § 300, Appendix A, Question 39). Specifically, an IEP team must ensure that a FBA is completed when, at a Manifestation Determination, they discover that a child who does not have a BIP will be removed from his or her current placement for more than 10 school days, regardless of whether the behavior was a manifestation of the child's disability (20 U.S.C. § 1415[k][1][D][ii]). If the student being removed from a placement already has a BIP, the IEP team must review the plan and modify it as necessary (20 U.S.C. § 1415[k][1][F]). IDEA and its regulations are silent on how a FBA must be conducted, but it must be individualized for each student. Finally, because FBAs are a form of evaluation, parent/guardian consent is required (34 CFR § 300.300[a] & [c]).

INTERIM ALTERNATIVE EDUCATIONAL SETTINGS

An Interim Alternative Educational Setting (IAES) placement is required when a student is removed from his or her IEP placement for more than 10 days. Essentially, an IAES placement is a temporary placement for a student with a disability who is suspended for more than 10 days. Although the removal of a student may be made unilaterally by school personnel or by a hearing officer, the IAES is determined by the IEP team. The team must identify where the student will be during the suspension, in order to ensure that the student can still make progress toward IEP goals and receive services. The IAES concept originated when zero tolerance policies became popular in schools. These policies usually involve immediate and long-term removal of students who supposedly jeopardize school safety. However, removing students with disabilities for a long period without attending to their procedural protections would be a violation of IDEA's guarantee of a Free Appropriate Public Education (FAPE). A student at an IAES must continue to receive educational services to enable the student to participate in the general education curriculum and to progress toward meeting IEP goals (34 CFR § 300.530[d][1]).

INTERIM ALTERNATIVE EDUCATIONAL SETTINGS. CONTINUED

An IAES can occur at a variety of settings, such as the child's home, an alternative school, or a residential facility placement. However, a district cannot offer home placement as the only option. While in the IAES placement, the student must continue to participate in the general education curriculum, receive special education services, and progress toward meeting IEP goals (U.S. Department of Education, 2009). Also, an FBA and BIP must occur because the student will be removed for more than 10 days. IAES placement for emergency removals must be no longer than 45 *school* days (20 U.S.C. § 1415[k][3][B][ii][II]).

UNIDENTIFIED STUDENTS WITH DISABILITIES

Students without an IEP or Section 504 Plan may still be entitled to a Manifestation Determination. This protection is triggered when a student is suspended for more than 10 days and the school has received notice that the student should have been identified as having a disability (20 U.S.C. § 1415[k][5][A] & [B]).

A school is considered to have notice that a student is protected by IDEA if:

1. the parent/guardian expressed concern in writing to administrators or the student's teacher(s) that the child is in need of special education and related services,
2. the parent/guardian requested an evaluation for the student, or
3. the student's teacher or other school personnel directly expressed specific concerns to the director of special education or to other supervisory personnel about the student's pattern of behavior (20 U.S.C. § 1415[k][5][A] & [B]).

Courts have found violations of IDEA when school districts disciplined students not yet identified as having disabilities. For example, an Ohio federal district court found that a school district erred when it failed to provide a Manifestation Determination before disciplining a 3rd- grader. Although the student did not have an Individualized Education Program (IEP), the court reasoned that the school had sufficient reason to suspect the student had a disability because the school had referred him to an outside mental health agency (*Jackson v. Northwest Local School District*, 2010).

After the groups are finished with scenarios or 15 minutes have elapsed, whichever comes first, the facilitator will identify the correct answers and rationales, detailed in the answer key for the discipline scenarios found in Table 6.2.

QUESTIONS FOR CONVERSATION (5–10 MINUTES)

Before the lesson, the facilitator will distribute the following questions to four different participants. The facilitator can ask the selected participants to ask the questions during the Legal Lesson, or may devote time after the Activity portion of the lesson for Q-and-A.

Table 6.2. Answer Key for the Discipline Scenarios

	Legal?	Illegal?
Andrew: Legal Support for Your Conclusion: Since Andrew possessed a weapon, the principal could remove him immediately. However, within 10 days, Andrew's IEP team must hold a Manifestation Determination. At this meeting, the IEP team would determine the IAES. The district could not limit the option solely to home placement. Also, Andrew cannot be at an IAES for longer than 45 school days, so a 3-month removal is problematic. Finally, the IEP team would discuss whether Andrew's misbehavior was caused by his hearing impairment, if his IEP was being properly implemented, and whether PBIS is needed.		X
Santiago: Legal Support for Your Conclusion: No, Santiago was an unidentified student with a disability. It is the school's responsibility to identify whether Santiago should be receiving special education and related services. Since Santiago's parents gave his teacher a note about his disability and previous IEP, the school was legally required to follow up on that information. Therefore, because the school had suspended Santiago for more than 10 days, he was entitled to a Manifestation Determination. Additionally, courts have determined that even students who did not have IEPs when the misbehavior occurred may still be entitled to a Manifestation Determination (*Jackson v. Northwest Local Sch. Dist.*, 2010; *Richland Sch. Dist. v. Thomas P.*, 2000).		X
Mona: Legal Support for Your Conclusion: Yes, the IEP team, not the principal, has the authority to determine whether a student's placement should be changed. An exception to this general rule occurs in emergency situations (e.g., if Mona had inflicted serious bodily injury). In all situations where a student is removed for more than 10 days, the IEP team is still required to convene within 10 days. Mona's IEP team properly reviewed whether her misconduct was related to her disability and whether her IEP was being properly implemented. Her IEP team was also following IDEA's requirements for PBIS when it scheduled an FBA.	X	
Isaac: Legal Support for Your Conclusion: No, the IEP team, not the principal, has the authority to determine whether a student's placement should be changed for more than 10 days. Because Isaac will be removed from his current placement for a total of 11 cumulative days, a Manifestation Determination must occur. Here, because Isaac did not cause serious bodily injury, possess a weapon, possess or use illegal drugs, or sell or solicit a controlled substance, the principal does not have unilateral authority to act, in contrast to the scenario with Andrew discussed earlier. Further, the Manifestation Determination must occur when a student with a disability is removed for a total of more than 10 days within a school year, if the repeated suspensions constitute a pattern of exclusion. In this situation, Isaac had been suspended two times for fighting; thus, the two brief suspensions occurred for similar behavior, suggesting a pattern that needs to be analyzed by his IEP team.		X
Zhong: Legal Support for Your Conclusion: Yes, it is up to the IEP team to review Zhong's discipline in light of his disability. Students with disabilities may be disciplined and removed from school for more than 10 days. It is important that special education and related services still be provided while the student is removed from the original placement. Zhong's removal lasting 11 cumulative days over the academic year is permissible. Because the incidents of misbehavior were similar, the IEP team was correct to conduct a Manifestation Determination. Even though Zhong's violence toward his teachers was not related to his specific learning disability, the IEP team also properly considered PBIS because Zhong has a history of problem behaviors, and it is likely that he will engage in this behavior again.	X	

1. If a student is removed to an IAES, does the district have to provide all the services in the IEP? It depends on what the individual student needs. The IDEA regulations emphasize that the student must continue to receive educational services that enable the student to continue to participate in the general education curriculum and progress toward meeting IEP goals. However, the district does not have to provide every service listed in the student's IEP. The IEP team determines the type and intensity of the services needed based on each individual student's needs. If the student is not progressing while in an IAES, the IEP team should review and revise the services and/or the IAES (U.S. Department of Education, 2009).

2. What constitutes serious bodily injury, weapons, or controlled substances that justify a student's immediate removal? The U.S. Department of Education has explicitly stated that local and state boards of education cannot use their own definition of serious bodily injury (U.S. Department of Education, 2009). Instead, the 2004 IDEA regulations define serious bodily injury as "bodily injury which involves (A) a substantial risk of death, (B) extreme physical pain, (C) protracted and obvious disfigurement, or (D) protracted loss or impairment of the function of a bodily member, organ, or mental faculty" (34 CFR § 300.530[i][3]). The serious bodily injury must occur "while at school, on school premises, or at a school function" (34 CFR § 300.530[g][1]-[3]). In one case, an elementary school student with autism kicked his principal in the knee and was removed to an IAES for inflicting serious bodily injury. However, his parents successfully challenged his removal because the district was unable to show that the principal's sharp knee pain constituted extreme physical pain (*Bisbee Unified Sch. Dist.*, 2010).

IDEA defines a weapon as a "weapon, device, instrument, material, or substance . . . that is used for, or is readily capable of, causing death or serious bodily injury" (34 CFR § 300.530[g][1]).

A controlled substance is a drug or other substance identified under schedules I, II, III, IV, or V in section 202(c) of the Controlled Substances Act (21 U.S.C. § 812[c], 1970). For example, controlled substances include heroin, marijuana, Ambien, and Robitussin AC (Drug Enforcement Agency, n.d.).

3. What occurs if the parents/guardians disagree with the rest of the IEP team about whether a child's behavior was or was not a manifestation of the child's disability? Similar to other placement disagreements in special education, the parents/guardians have the right to appeal and request a hearing (34 CFR § 300.532[a]). The hearing must occur within 20 school days. During the hearing process, the student must stay in an IAES for no longer than 45 days unless the parents and the local or state education agency decide otherwise (34 CFR § 300.533). The hearing officer has 10 days to issue a decision once the hearing has been completed.

4. What is the difference between discipline procedures for students who are eligible for services under IDEA (and have IEPs) and discipline procedures for students who are eligible for services under Section 504 (and have Section 504 Plans)? There are similarities and differences. The 10-Day Rule requirement to hold a Manifestation Determination applies to students receiving services under both IDEA and Section 504. Similar to an IEP team, the Section 504 committee must meet to evaluate whether the student's behavior was substantially related to his/her disability.

Unlike the IDEA, however, Section 504 does not require the district to provide educational services during the suspension of a student that results from the student's behavior.

TEST YOUR KNOWLEDGE (5–10 MINUTES)

The facilitator will give each participant an index card and ask them to write down at least three legal violations that occur in the following skit. Facilitators can act out the skit or request that five participants perform it. After the participants have responded on the index cards, the facilitator will review the participants' responses to ascertain whether the participants mastered the objectives.

The participants should identify the following legal violations:

- No Manifestation Determination occurred, so the 10-Day Rule was violated because the student will be removed from placement for a total of 13 days.
- No serious bodily injury occurred and, therefore, the principal did not have the authority to unilaterally impose the immediate removal of the student.
- The school did not implement PBIS even though the student will be removed for more than 10 days.
- The parents/guardians would not ask for a BIP; instead, the school should provide a FBA that would then result in a BIP.
- The student will miss a science test and speech therapy, which indicates that he is not being provided his special education and related services as required under IDEA.

Legal Violations Skit

Two students, Alex and Sean, are pushing one another.

Teacher: Okay, break it up! Break it up!
Students stop fighting.
Teacher: Come with me to the principal's office!
Alex: Aw, Mrs./Mr. Miller, no one even got hurt, can't you just give us a detention?
Teacher: Absolutely not. We do not tolerate fighting in our school!
Alex, Sean, and Teacher exit.
Principal and Parent enter.

Principal: Thank you for coming to pick up Alex, Mr./Mrs. Smith. He will be suspended for 5 days for fighting.

Parent: Five days? Alex was already suspended 8 days for fighting this year! He also has an important science test that he can't miss tomorrow. You know, I think Alex got in a fight because he is so impulsive and has trouble communicating. At his last IEP meeting, I mentioned that something needs to be done about his behavior. Each year, it's getting worse.

Principal: That very well may be. However, we do not tolerate fighting at this school. You can ask for a BIP at next year's IEP meeting, but for now, Alex will be suspended immediately. In order to improve Alex's behavior he needs to know that the discipline policies apply to him just like everyone else!

Parent: But what about his science test? If he misses it, he's going to fail that class!

Principal: Again, we have to show Alex that there are consequences for his bad behavior. Maybe when he misses that test, he'll think before he fights next time.

Parent: He also has speech therapy scheduled in a few days. Can't he at least come in for that?

Principal: No, sorry. When fighting is involved, it is my responsibility to remove the student immediately from our school, even if the student has an IEP.

ADDITIONAL RESOURCES

Center for Effective Collaboration and Practice. *Functional behavioral assessment.* Retrieved from http://cecp.air.org/fba/

Council for Exceptional Children. *Webinar resources.* Retrieved from http://www.cec.sped.org/Professional-Development/Webinars/Recorded-Webinars

Council of Parent Attorneys and Advocates. *Unsafe in the schoolhouse: Abuse of children with disabilities.* Retrieved from http://www.copaa.org/wp-content/uploads/2010/10/ UnsafeCOPAAMay_27_2009.pdf

Office of Special Education Programs (OSEP) technical assistance center on positive behavioral interventions and supports. Retrieved from http://www.pbis.org/ pbis_resource_detail_page.aspx?PBIS_ResourceID=906

Resources on positive Behavioral Interventions and Functional Behavior Assessments. Retrieved from http://www.edlawrc.com/ pbis.html

School Policies on Physical Restraints. Retrieved from http://www.edlawrc.com/sample_policies_on_physical_rest.htm

U.S. Department of Education. (n.d.). *IDEA discipline.* Retrieved from file:///C:/Users/deckerjr/Downloads/Discipline%208-23-06%20Final.pdf

U.S. Department of Education. (2009). *Questions and answers on discipline procedures.* Retrieved from http://idea.ed.gov/explore/view/p/%2Croot%2Cdynamic%2CQaCorner%2C7%2C

U.S. Department of Education. (2012). *Restraint and seclusion: Resource document.* Retrieved from http://www2.ed.gov/policy/seclusion/restraints-and-seclusion-resources.pdf

REFERENCES

Bisbee Unified Sch. Dist., No. 2, 54 IDELR 39 (SEA AZ, 2010).

Butler, J. (2012). *How safe is the schoolhouse? An analysis of state restraint and seclusion policies.* Retrieved from http://www.autcom.org/pdf/howsafeschoolhouse.pdf

Controlled Substances Act, 21 U.S.C. § 812(c) (1970).

Drug Enforcement Agency (n.d.). *Drug scheduling.* Retrieved from http://www.dea.gov/druginfo/ds.shtml

Fantz, A. (2008, December 17). *Children forced into cell-like school seclusion rooms.* Retrieved from http://www.cnn.com/2008/US/12/17/seclusion.rooms/index.html

Honig v. Doe, 484 U.S. 305 (1988).

Individuals with Disabilities Education Act, 20 U.S.C. § 1400 et seq. (2004).

Individuals with Disabilities Education Act, Part B Regulations, 34 C.F.R. §§ 300.530-536 (2006).

Jackson v. Northwest Local School District, 2010 WL 3452333 (S.D. Ohio, 2010).

J.P.M. v. Palm Beach Cnty. Sch. Bd., 916 F.Supp.2d 1314 (S.D. FL. 2013).

Katsiyannis, A., Losinski, M., & Prince, A. M. T. (2012). Litigation and students with disabilities: A persistent concern. *NASSP Bulletin, 95*(1), 1–21.

Keeping All Students Safe Act (KASSA), H.R. 1893 (2013).

King v. Pioneer Reg'l Educ. Serv. Agency, 688 S.E.2d 7 (Ga. App. 2009).

Metro. Bd. of Pub. Educ. v. Bellamy, 116 F. App'x 570 (6th Cir. 2004).

Richland Sch. Dist. v. Thomas P., 2000 U.S. Dist. Lexis 15162 (W.D. Wis. 2000).

TASH. (2011). The cost of waiting. Retrieved from http://tash.org/wp-content/uploads/2011/04/TASH_The-Cost-of-Waiting_April-2011.pdf

U.S. Department of Education. (2009). *Questions and answers on discipline procedures.* Retrieved from http://idea.ed.gov/explore/view/p/%2Croot%2Cdynamic%2CQaCorner%2C7%2C

U.S. Government Accountability Office. (2009). *Seclusions and restraints: Selected cases of death and abuse at public and private schools and treatment centers* (GAO-09-719T). Retrieved from http://www.gao.gov/assets/130/122526.pdf

Williams, J. L., Pazey, B., Shelby, L., & Yates, J. R. (2013). The enemy among us: Do school administrators perceive students with disabilities as a threat? *NASSP Bulletin, 97*(2), 139–165.

Why Must We Plan for Students' Lives Beyond High School?

INTRODUCTION FOR FACILITATORS

Educators and parents are concerned about future educational, employment, and independent adult living plans for students with disabilities once they complete high school. An increasing number of them are enrolled in postsecondary education, including community colleges and 4-year colleges and universities; they are also pursuing fulfilling careers immediately after high school (Rothstein & Johnson, 2010). Despite these encouraging trends, however, a survey revealed that 4 out of 10 parents of students with disabilities believed that their children's special education programs were failing or needed improvement in terms of preparing their children for adult life beyond high school (Johnson & Duffett, 2002). Therefore, there is a clear need to address the transition period from high school to adulthood for students with disabilities.

In 2004, Congress reauthorized the IDEA requiring that transition services be included in a student's IEP by the time the student reaches 16 years old, or sooner if determined appropriate by the IEP team. For instance, many students with disabilities begin transition services as early as middle school based on required coursework if they plan to pursue any type of postsecondary education (Prince, Katsiyannis, & Farmer, 2013).

Additionally, the 2004 IDEA reauthorization added two provisions involving transition services. First, a student must now be invited to attend any IEP meeting where the purpose of the meeting involves the "consideration of postsecondary goals" (34 CFR § 300.321[b]). Second, after obtaining parental consent, the school should invite a representative from any participating agency that is responsible for providing or paying for a student's transition services to attend the student's IEP meeting (34 CFR § 300.321[b][3]).

Transition services are defined under the IDEA as a coordinated set of activities for a student with a disability that:

1. Is designed to be within a results-oriented process; that is, focused on improving the academic and functional achievement of the child with a

disability to facilitate the child's movement from school to postschool activities, including postsecondary education, vocational education, integrated employment (including supported employment), continuing and adult education, adult services, independent living, or community participation;
2. Is based on the individual child's needs, taking into account the child's strengths, preferences, and interests; and
3. Includes instruction, related services, community experiences, the development of employment and other postschool adult living objectives, and, when appropriate, acquisition of daily living skills and functional vocational evaluation (20 U.S.C. § 1401[34]).

MATERIALS NEEDED

- Internet connection, projector, and screen to show video (see *Activity*);
- Facilitator script(s) (see *Background, Purpose, and Objectives*);
- Either a whiteboard with dry-erase markers or 4 large sheets of paper and markers for the Beyond High School Brainstorming Exercise (see *Hook*);
- Beyond High School Brainstorming Exercise Answer Sheet handout (one for each participant) (see *Hook*);
- Student Transition Services Under the IDEA: Student Scenario (one for each participant) (see *Activity*);
- Transition Services and Post–High School Goals Activity handout (one for each participant) (see *Activity*);
- Transition Services and Post–High School Goals Activity: Sample Responses handout (one for each participant) (see *Activity*);
- Questions for Conversation (typed or written) (see *Questions for Conversation*);
- National Secondary Transition Technical Assistance Center (NSTTAC) Indicator 13 Checklist for developing a legally compliant IEP that includes appropriate transition services (one for each participant) (see *Test Your Knowledge*); and
- Optional: Objectives visually displayed (see *Background, Purpose, and Objectives*).

HOOK (15 MINUTES)

Beyond High School Brainstorming Exercise

To begin the lesson, the facilitator will choose three participants to come to the front of the room to lead the larger group in a brainstorming exercise while the remaining participants observe and assist by calling out possible answers.

Each of the three participants will be assigned to either a whiteboard with dry-erase markers or one of the three pieces of large paper. Each of the following three categories will be written on either a section of the whiteboard board or one of the three pieces of paper:

1. Postsecondary Education;
2. Employment and Career Training;
3. Adult Independent Living Skills.

The facilitator will instruct the three participants that they are to identify as many examples of activities as possible associated with their assigned category. For instance, under Adult Independent Living Skills, an example could be "shopping for groceries." The three participants will seek assistance from the other participants in the audience. After the participants have identified some possibilities, the facilitator will distribute a handout detailing possible responses under each of the three categories to each of the participants. The facilitator will ask the participants whether or not their responses matched any on the handout:

Postsecondary Education

1. 4-year college or university
2. Community college
3. Private school
4. Adult vocational or technical school

Employment and Career Training

1. Vocational career assessment or evaluation
2. Community-based job exploration
3. Paid work experiences
4. Apprenticeships
5. Part-time employment in chosen career field prior to high school graduation
6. Military

Adult Independent Living Skills

1. Money and management skills
2. Residential living skills
3. Knowledge of mobility/transportation options
4. Communication skills
5. Social relationships
6. Self-medication, health, and safety
7. Knowledge of community resources (banks, post office, shopping, libraries, etc.)

At the completion of the Beyond High School Brainstorming Exercise, the facilitator will explain that the purpose of this exercise is to encourage the participants to begin thinking about the wide array of post–high school transition options available to students with disabilities.

BACKGROUND, PURPOSE, AND OBJECTIVES OF THE LESSON (5 MINUTES)

Next, the facilitator will read the following **Facilitator Script,** or discuss something similar with the participants (if there is more than one facilitator, you may choose to split the script among them). The facilitator should consider having the Objectives displayed visually so that the participants can refer to them during the lesson.

Facilitators: Today's lesson will focus on student transition under the IDEA. An IEP team must follow specific steps to plan for a student's transition from high school to adult life. When IEP teams develop transition plans, they ensure that schools are directing their special education and related services to employment, postsecondary education, and/or independent adult living skills.

The specific objectives for today's lesson are for participants to:

1. Define "transition services" under the IDEA,
2. Recognize the importance of maintaining a continuation of services beyond high school and into adulthood for students with disabilities,
3. Understand that the IDEA requires the inclusion of transition planning in each child's IEP by the time a student reaches the age of 16 (if not before), and
4. Explain that transition planning must include both the student's academic achievement and functional performance and recommendations to assist the students in meeting any postsecondary goals.

ACTIVITY (30 MINUTES)

To begin this lesson, the facilitator will ask the participants to view the 8-minute video about creating an IEP available here: http://www.youtube.com/watch?v=FCNDWWCdq0M. This video provides instruction in writing a post–high school or postsecondary goal for a student with disabilities, which is required for transition services on a student's IEP. After the video is over, ask the participants to share their thoughts about the video with other participants in the group.

Next, the facilitators will divide the participants into small groups of three or four. Each small group will comprise a separate IEP team. At this time, the facilitator will distribute to each group a brief scenario of a student named Juanita with disabilities. Each IEP team shall consider appropriate, measurable post–high school or postsecondary goals in the areas of education, training, employment, and, if necessary, adult independent living skills.

Student Transition Services Under IDEA: Student Scenario

Juanita is a 16-year-old high school student with a moderate cognitive disability. She will graduate from high school in several months. For the last 2 years, Juanita has worked at a small concession stand at a local movie theater about 20 hours each week. Juanita regularly goes to a local mall with her friends, and participates in several activities at her high school.

While Juanita enjoys her work at the concession stand, she would prefer to work at a restaurant. She thinks working at a restaurant in a large city would be exciting, but she currently does not have the skills to be a cook. Juanita expressed her desire to acquire new skills to reach her goal of working in a downtown restaurant located about an hour away from her home. Additionally, Juanita has expressed her desire to apply for jobs working for a large fast-food restaurant chain to gain experience working in the restaurant industry.

Juanita's parents have expressed concern that she needs more training and skill development to become prepared for the adult workplace. Also, Juanita currently reads at a 6th-grade level and sometimes experiences difficulties reading signs in unfamiliar places.

Facilitator: As members of the IEP team, you need to develop appropriate, measurable postsecondary goals based on the information provided in the scenario we have given you, which describes a student requiring transition services under the IDEA. The facilitators should provide the Transition Services and Post–High School Goals Exercise handout (Figure 7.1) to the participants.

The Facilitators should then instruct the IEP teams that they each have 15 minutes to first discuss the student scenarios, and then develop what each IEP team considers to be appropriate post—high school goals in the areas of education and training, employment, and independent living.

After each IEP team has completed writing down possible post—high school goals based on the student scenarios, the Facilitators should distribute to each IEP team the handout (Figure 7.2) of possible post–high school goals for their assigned students in each of the areas of education and training, employment, and independent living.

QUESTIONS FOR CONVERSATION (5–10 MINUTES)

Before the lesson, the facilitator will distribute the following questions to two different participants. The facilitator will ask them to ask the questions either during the Legal Lesson or after the Activity portion of the lesson for Q-and-A.

The two questions are:

Figure 7.1. Student Scenario: Juanita—Transition Services and Post-High School Goals Exercise Handout

Based on the scenario, what are some goals the IEP team should consider for Juanita in the following areas?

Education and Training Goal(s):

Employment Goal(s):

Independent Living Goal(s):

Figure 7.2. Student Scenario: Juanita—Transition Services and Post-High School Goals Exercise: Sample Responses Handout

Is there an appropriate measurable postsecondary goal(s) that covers education or training, employment, and, as needed, independent living?

Education and Training Goal(s):

Goal 1: After graduating high school, Juanita will attend a technical college and participate in a culinary arts industry certificate program, thus meeting the requirements necessary to enter the food service industry.

Goal 2: After graduating high school, Juanita will attend courses at least twice a week at a community college designed to provide specialized academic, functional, and occupational preparation for individuals with disabilities.

Employment Goal(s):

Goal 1: After graduating high school, Juanita will access public transportation to get to and from work each day.

Goal 2: After graduating high school, Juanita will work 20 hours per week at a local restaurant with temporary supports through vocational rehabilitation.

Independent Living Goal(s):

Goal 1: After graduating high school, Juanita will independently prepare for work each day, including dressing, making her bed, and making her lunch.

Goal 2: After graduating from high school, Juanita will live semi-independently with a roommate and with supports.

1. What kind of special education and related services are students with disabilities eligible to receive in a post-high school environment? There are a variety of special education and related services available to students with disabilities post–high school. It is critical to determine the student's postsecondary plans. Three primary areas of consideration for students with disabilities beyond high school include postsecondary education, employment and career training, and/or adult independent living. For example, a student with disabilities who is planning to live independently would need assistance with money management skills and communication skills. Some examples of employment and career training for a student with disabilities transitioning from high school would include community-based job exploration assistance, vocational career assessment, or apprenticeships.

2. What if the IEP team disagrees with the career choice of the parent/guardian and child? It is important that parents/guardians and school officials have collaborative and candid discussions involving the career choice(s) of the child. If the IEP team disagrees with the parents/guardians, it is critical that both sides work closely to foster mutual collaboration. The ultimate goal in determining a suitable career choice for a student with disabilities is a choice that is based on the "best interest(s) of the child." The IDEA encourages parental participation in the IEP process, and the IEP team must work closely with both the student and parents/guardians to arrive at a mutually acceptable decision.

TEST YOUR KNOWLEDGE (5 MINUTES)

The facilitator will distribute to the participants a checklist listing eight questions that each IEP team must address in order to legally comply with the IDEA requirement of including transition services in a student's IEP.

Table 7.1. National Secondary Transition Technical Assistance Center (NSTTAC) Indicator Checklist

	POSTSECONDARY GOALS		
Questions	*Education/ Training*	*Employment*	*Independent Living*
1. Is there an appropriate measurable postsecondary goal or goals in this area? Can the goal(s) be counted? Will the goal(s) occur after the student graduates from school? Based on the information available about this student, does (do) the postsecondary goal(s) seem appropriate for this student? • If yes to all three, then circle Y OR if a postsecondary goal(s) is (are) not stated, circle N	Y N	Y N	Y N NA
2. Is (are) the postsecondary goal(s) updated annually? Was (were) the postsecondary goal(s) addressed/ updated in conjunction with the development of the current IEP? • If yes, then circle Y OR If the postsecondary goal(s) was (were) not updated with the current IEP, circle N	Y N	Y N	Y N NA
3. Is there evidence that the measurable postsecondary goal(s) were based on age appropriate transition assessment? Is the use of transition assessment(s) for the postsecondary goal(s) mentioned in the IEP or evident in the student's file? • If yes, then circle Y OR if no, then circle N	Y N	Y N	Y N
4. Are there transition services in the IEP that will reasonably enable the student to meet his or her postsecondary goal(s)? Is a type of instruction, related service, community experience, or development of employment and other post-school adult living objectives, and if appropriate, acquisition of daily living skills, and provision of a functional vocational evaluation listed in association with meeting the post-secondary goal(s)? • If yes, then circle Y OR if no, then circle N	Y N	Y N	Y N
5. Do the transition services include courses of study that will reasonably enable the student to meet his or her postsecondary goal(s)? Do the transition services include courses of study that align with the student's postsecondary goal(s)? • If yes, then circle Y OR if no, then circle N	Y N	Y N	Y N

Table 7.1. National Secondary Transition Technical Assistance Center (NSTTAC) Indicator Checklist, Continued

Questions	POSTSECONDARY GOALS *Education/ Training*	*Employment*	*Independent Living*
6. Is (are) there annual IEP goal(s) related to the student's transition services needs?	Y N	Y N	Y N
Is (are) an annual goal(s) included in the IEP that is/are related to the student's transition services needs? • If yes, then circle Y OR if no, then circle N			
7. Is there evidence that the student was invited to the IEP Team meeting where transition services were discussed?	Y N	Y N	Y N
For the current year, is there documented evidence in the IEP or cumulative folder that the student was invited to attend the IEP Team meeting? • If yes, then circle Y OR if no, then circle N			
8. If appropriate, is there evidence that a representative of any participating agency was invited to the IEP Team meeting with the prior consent of the parent or student who has reached the age of majority?	Y N	Y N	Y N
For the current year, is there evidence in the IEP that representatives of any of the following agencies/services were invited to participate in the IEP development including but not limited to: postsecondary education, vocational education, integrated employment (including supported employment), continuing and adult education, adult services, independent living or community participation for this post-secondary goal? Was consent obtained from the parent (or student, for a student the age of majority)? • If yes to both, then circle Y • If no invitation is evident and a participating agency is likely to be responsible for providing or paying for transition services and there was consent to invite them to the IEP meeting, then circle N • If it is too early to determine if the student will need outside agency involvement, or no agency is likely to provide or pay for transition services, circle NA • If parent or individual student consent (when appropriate) was not provided, circle NA			

Does the IEP meet the requirements of Indicator 13? (Circle one)

Yes (all Ys or NAs for each item [1-8] on the checklist included in the IEP are circled) Or No (one or more Ns circled)

Source: National Secondary Transition Technical Assistance Center (NSTTAC).

The facilitator will ask the participants to first review the eight questions posed in Table 7.1, and then write on index cards the one question they believe to be the most difficult to answer involving transition services for a student with disabilities.

ADDITIONAL RESOURCES

National Secondary Transition Technical Assistance Center (NSTTAC). Available at http://www.nsttac.org

Wrightslaw. *Transition, transition services, transition planning*. Available at http://www.wrightslaw.com/info/ trans.index.htm

REFERENCES

Individuals with Disabilities Education Act, 20 U.S.C. § 1400 et seq. (2004).

Johnson, J., & Duffett, A. (2002). When it's your own child: A report on special education from the families who use it. New York, NY: Public Agenda.

National Secondary Transition Technical Assistance Center (NSTTAC), Retrieved from http://www.findyouthinfo.gov/content/national-secondary-transition-technical-assistance-center

Prince, A., Katsiyannis, A., & Farmer, J. (2013). Postsecondary transition under IDEA 2004: A legal update. *Intervention in School and Clinic, 48*(5), 286–293.

Rothstein, L., & Johnson, S.F. (2010). *Special education law.* Thousand Oaks, CA: SAGE.

Why Is Fostering Positive Family-School Relationships Important?

INTRODUCTION FOR FACILITATORS

There is considerable evidence supporting the theory that students' learning and other educational outcomes improve when school officials and families work together (Henderson & Mapp, 2002). Cooperative family and school relationships are important to the process of developing effective program plans and services for students with disabilities, delivering these services, and properly communicating the students' progress in school. The breakdown of these relationships can negatively impact the quality of these programs and result in a significant loss of time and money for both parents and schools (Andren, 2010). Finding effective and efficient ways to manage special education disputes while simultaneously supporting positive family-school relationships is an issue of growing concern (Nowell & Salem, 2007). A 2014 study by the U.S. General Accounting Office (GAO) highlights the need for improved and more transparent data on the level of parental involvement in special education disputes (U.S. General Accounting Office, 2014). For over 3 decades, parents/guardians and schools have spent millions of dollars attempting to resolve special education disputes. In its 2004 reauthorization, the IDEA actively encourages more collaborative and conciliatory approaches to reconciling conflicts between parents/guardians and schools. These approaches include mediation, due process complaints, and the resolution process referred to as alternative dispute resolution (ADR). ADR methods often provide more effective and efficient ways to address special education disagreements between parents/guardians and school officials before the disputes become more costly and time-consuming lawsuits (Mueller, 2009).

MATERIALS NEEDED

- Questions for conversation on note cards (see *Background, Purpose, and Objectives*);

- Top Ten Methods to Foster IEP Team Collaboration handout (see *Background, Purpose, and Objectives*);
- A.G. Bell Association successful collaborative IEP video on YouTube (see *Activity*);
- Alternative Dispute Resolution Processes Comparison Chart handout (see *Activity*);
- Procedural Safeguards: Parents' Right to Participate in the IEP Process of Their Child handout (see *Test Your Knowledge*); and
- Optional: Objectives visually displayed (see *Background, Purpose, and Objectives*).

HOOK (10–15 MINUTES)

To begin this lesson, the facilitator will introduce a case scenario titled Parental Participation and Scheduling an IEP Meeting, shown below, dramatizing a dispute between school members of an IEP team and one child's parents. This scenario involves a dispute over the scheduling of an IEP meeting at which a significant change was made to the student's IEP without the presence of the parents at the meeting. The participants will read the brief scenario, and the facilitators will lead a discussion concerning what the participants view as options to effectively resolve the dispute without formal legal action. At the end of the discussion, the facilitator will explain that the case scenario they just read actually happened and is based on a 2013 legal case, *Doug C. v. State of Hawaii Dep't of Educ.* (2013), where the U.S. Court of Appeals for the Ninth Circuit ruled that the failure to include the parents at an IEP meeting violated a procedural requirement of the IDEA, and therefore invalidated the student's IEP.

Case Scenario: Parental Participation and Scheduling an IEP Meeting

Maya is a 16-year-old high school student, who was diagnosed with autism at age 2 and has been eligible for special education and related services under the IDEA since that time. At the beginning of 5th grade, Maya's IEP team recommended that she attend a private school specializing in the provision of special education and related services for children with autism. According to Maya's IEP, her private education was to be paid for by the public school district she originally attended.

Earlier this month, Maya's IEP team held a meeting at which the team changed her placement from her current private school to the local public high school. Maya's parents, Debra and Larry, were unable to attend this particular IEP meeting due to a scheduling conflict. According to other IEP members, numerous unsuccessful attempts were made to schedule an IEP meeting based on the parents' availability. The IEP team responded by presenting two additional dates for Maya's parents to consider. Maya's father said that he could possibly attend one of these meetings, but could not fully commit since he was ill, and could not guarantee that he would recover in time for the IEP meeting. Then the IEP team suggested that both parents participate in the meeting by phone or teleconference through the Internet. However, both parents insisted that they wanted to be physically present at Maya's IEP meeting. Debra and Larry are now very upset that they were excluded from the IEP team meeting and informed the IEP team that they are considering legal action against the school district, because the IEP meeting was held without their consent, and they were not present to discuss a major change (i.e., the change in placement) to Maya's IEP.

BACKGROUND, PURPOSE, AND OBJECTIVES OF THE LESSON (10 MINUTES)

Next, the facilitator will introduce the topic by reading the following **Facilitator Script.** The facilitator should consider displaying the objectives visually, so that the participants can refer to them during the lesson.

Facilitators: Today's lesson will discuss the importance of positive family-school relationships in the Individualized Education Program (IEP) process. The successful development and implementation of IEPs is best facilitated by a cooperative relationship between school officials and the parents/guardians of a student with a disability. Specifically, the IDEA legally requires that parents/guardians serve as members of the IEP team, and encourages their active participation. In addition, the IDEA provides many legal rights to each parent/guardian of a child with disabilities, including notification of such rights parental consent prior to an initial evaluation, the right to a reevaluation, and the ability to contest decisions about the child's education through mediation or a due process hearing (Bartlett, Etschedidt, & Weisenstein, 2007).

The specific objectives for today's lesson are:

1. Identify common problem areas in facilitating family-school relationships related to the special education process.
2. Describe current alternative dispute resolution procedures, including facilitated IEP meetings, resolution sessions, mediation, and due process hearings, as ways to more effectively address legal conflicts in the special education process.

ACTIVITY (30 MINUTES)

Fostering IEP Team Collaboration Exercise

The facilitators will introduce an exercise aimed at improving collaboration among IEP members. For this portion of the lesson, the facilitator will pass out the handout, Top Ten Methods to Foster IEP Team Collaboration (Figure 8.1) and play a 7-minute video (provided by the A.G. Bell Association) that

Figure 8.1. Top Ten Methods to Foster IEP Team Collaboration

1. Build trust and create relationships.
2. Put aside egos; everyone is equal.
3. Share a goal.
4. Share accountability.
5. Become an active listener.
6. Make communication easy.
7. Be open to other team members' ideas.
8. Know the team's strengths and limitations.
9. Use creative and critical thinking.
10. Stop making offers; make group decisions instead.

Source: Doug Goldberg, Special Education Advisor Blog, http://www.specialeducationadvisor.com/top-ten-methods-to-foster-iep-team-collaboration/

shows an example of a noncollaborative IEP meeting. The video is available at https://www.youtube.com/watch?v=Pu4KnwNu1Rw. After watching this, the facilitators should encourage discussion around what specific ways this IEP meeting could be more collaborative. After a 10-minute discussion, the Facilitators will play a 12-minute video that shows an example of a successful and collaborative IEP meeting. The video is available at https://www.youtube.com/watch?v=d44wPE9azXk

The participants will then discuss the video for 10 minutes, focusing their attention on specific ways school members of the IEP team can use more effective communication strategies with parents.

After completing the exercise, the facilitator will select three participants to read aloud the common questions for conversation to the entire group. At this point, the facilitator should pass out the handout Alternative Dispute Resolution Processes Comparison Chart (Table 8.1).

QUESTIONS FOR CONVERSATION (5–10 MINUTES)

Before the lesson, the facilitator will distribute the following questions to three different participants. The facilitator will request that the three participants ask the questions either during the Legal Lesson or after the Activity portion of the lesson for Q-and-A.

1. What is alternative dispute resolution (ADR), and why do you think we need it for dealing with special education disputes between school officials and parents/guardians? Alternative dispute resolution, commonly referred to as ADR, is defined as any means used for resolving a dispute outside of a courtroom. In the context of special education legal disputes, ADR is mainly used to refer to alternatives to the more formal and legal due process administrative hearing. ADR is important because it offers parents/guardians and school officials the opportunity to resolve disputes collaboratively and to avoid costly litigation.

Table 8.1. Alternative Dispute Resolution Processes Comparison Chart Handout

Alternative Dispute Resolution Type	Mediation	Due Process Complaint	Resolution Process	State Complaint
Who can initiate the process?	Parent/guardian or school district, but must be voluntary for either.	Parent/guardian or school district.	School district schedules the resolution meeting upon receipt of a due process complaint unless the parties agree to waive it or use mediation.	Any individual or organization including those from out of state.
What is the time limit for filing?	None specified	Within 2 years of when the party knew or should have known of the problem.	Triggered by a parent/guardian's due process complaint.	One year from the date of the alleged violation.
What issues can be resolved?	Any matter, including matters arising prior to the filing of a due process complaint.	Any matter relating to the identification, evaluation, educational placement, or provision of a free appropriate public education.	Same as the issues raised in the parent/guardian's due process complaint.	Alleged violations of Part B of IDEA or Part 300.
What is the timeline for resolving the issues?	None specified.	45 days from the end of the resolution period, unless specific extensions to the timeline are granted.	School district must convene a resolution meeting within 15 days of receipt of the parent/guardian's due process complaint, unless the parties agree in writing to waive the meeting or agree to use mediation.	60 days from receipt of the complaint, unless an extension is permitted.
Who resolves the issues?	Parent/guardian and school district with a mediator. The process is voluntary, and both parties must agree to a resolution.	Hearing officer.	Parent/guardian and school district. Both parties must agree to a resolution.	State educational agency (SEA).

Source: U.S. Department of Education (2013) Office of Special Education Programs (OSEP) IDEA Dispute Resolution Processes Comparison Chart. Retrieved from http://www.directionservice.org/cadre/pdf/OSEP%20Comparison%20Chart%20FINAL%2011-2013.pdf

Figure 8.2. Thirteen Legal Rights of Parents to Participate in the IEP Process of Their Child

1. Right to independent educational evaluations.
2. Right to written notice.
3. Right to require parental consent.
4. Right to access their child's educational records.
5. Right to present and resolve complaints through the due process and state complaint procedures, including a timeline for filing a complaint, the opportunity to resolve the complaint, and the differences between the two processes (such as jurisdiction or authority, issues covered, filing and decisional timelines, and relevant procedures).
6. The right to the availability of mediation.
7. The right to the child's placement while any due process complaint is pending.
8. The right to procedures for students who are subject to placement in an interim alternative educational setting.
9. The right to know the requirements for parents who place their child in a private school at public expense.
10. The right to hearings on due process complaints, including requirements that evaluation results and recommendations be disclosed.
11. The right to state-level appeals.
12. The right to civil actions, including the time period in which to file those actions.
13. The right to attorneys' fees.

Source: National Dissemination Center for Children with Disabilities., Retrieved from http://www.parentcenterhub.org/wp-content/uploads/repo_items/qa2.pdf.

2. In your opinion, which of the ADR processes best satisfies the goal of fostering positive family-school relationships? (The facilitator asks the participants to refer to the handout "Alternative Dispute Resolution Processes Comparison Chart" and discuss the outlined alternative dispute resolution types, including mediation, due process complaints, resolution process, and state complaints).

3. What are the benefits of a positive collaborative relationship with parents/guardians when encountering special education disputes? There is considerable evidence detailing the benefits of cooperative family and school relationships involving special education disputes, especially in terms of avoiding costly and time-consuming lawsuits. The 2004 reauthorization of the IDEA actively encourages collaborative and conciliatory approaches between schools and families toward reconciling special education disputes, including mediation, due process complaints, and alternative dispute resolution.

TEST YOUR KNOWLEDGE (5 MINUTES)

The facilitator will distribute to the participants a handout listing 13 legal rights of parents/guardians to participate in the IEP processes of their children (Figure 8.2).

The facilitator will ask the participants to do a 5-minute Quick Write during which they write down the rights they believe best foster positive family relations and several specific strategies a school could use if they believe the relationship with a family during a special education dispute is becoming difficult.

ADDITIONAL RESOURCES

Family Empowerment and Disability Council WestEd Center for Prevention and Early Intervention. (2012). *The Individuals with Disabilities Education Act and Parent Participation*. Retrieved from http://www.calfedc.org/uploads/3/2/6/6/3266057/fedc_issue_brief_june_2012.pdf

National Center on Dispute Resolution in Special Education. (2010). *Nick Martin—21 best practices for successful IEPs*. Retrieved from http://www.directionservice.org/cadre/martinvid.cfm

National Center for Learning Disabilities. Retrieved from http://www.ncld.org

National Dissemination Center for Children with Disabilities (NICHCY). (2009). Questions and answers about IDEA: Parent participation. Retrieved from http://www.parentcenterhub.org/wpcontent/uploads/repo_items/qa2.pdf

Office of Dispute Resolution. *Videos*. Retrieved from http://odr-pa.org/parents/parent-resource-library/videos/

REFERENCES

Andren, K. (2010, January 10). School districts spend thousands on litigation over special education. *The Patriot News*. Retrieved from http://www.pennlive.com/midstate/index.ssf/2010/01/school_districts_spend_thousan.html

Bartlett, L. D., Etscheditt, S., & Weisenstein, G. R. (2007). *Special education law and practice in public schools* (2nd. ed.). Upper Saddle River, NJ: Pearson.

Doug C. v. State of Hawaii Dep't. of Educ., No. 12-15079 (9th Cir. 2013).

Henderson, A. T., & Mapp, K. L. (2002). *A new wave of evidence: The impact of school, family, and community connections on student achievement*. Retrieved from http://www.sedi.org/connections/resources/evidence.pdf

Individuals with Disabilities Education Act, 20 U.S.C. §§ 1400 *et seq.*, 34 C.F.R. §§ 200 *et seq*

Mueller, T. G. (2009, June). Alternative dispute resolution: A new agenda for special education policy. *Journal of Disability Policy Studies, 20*(1), 4–13.

Nowell, B. L., & Salem, D. A. (2007, September/October). The impact of special education mediation on parent-school relationships: Parents' perspective. *Remedial and Special Education, 28*(5), 304–315.

United States General Accounting Office. (2014). *Improved performance measures could enhance oversight of dispute resolution* (Report Number GAO 14-390). Retrieved from http://www.gao.gov/assets/670/ 665434.pdf

What Is the Basic Legal Framework Related to Students with Disabilities?

Educators need to know the basic framework of the U.S. legal system because almost every decision they make related to special education involves the law. Although education is traditionally considered a role of state government, the federal government is substantially more involved in education policy today than in the past. The word "education" does not appear in the U.S. Constitution and nothing in the Constitution requires that Congress enact laws governing education. Yet, Congress has passed many federal education laws, such as the Individuals with Disabilities Education Act (IDEA). So, how is this possible?

State legislatures do have primary authority to enact education laws (McCarthy, Cambron-McCabe, & Eckes, 2014, pp. 7–9). However, Congress has authority to provide funding and other regulations to schools through provisions found in the U.S. Constitution such as the Taxing and Spending, Commerce, and Obligation of Contracts clauses. Laws like the IDEA Act were enacted under the Taxing and Spending Clause to promote the general welfare of the nation. In order to receive federal funding, states agree to abide by the terms of federal laws such as the IDEA. In addition, individuals such as public school employees and students have certain rights outlined by the Constitution. Since the U.S. Constitution is the supreme law of the land that everyone must follow, it has significant influence over what occurs in schools. In sum, the federal government, including the U.S. Department of Education, federal judges, and Congress, are incredibly influential in determining how public schools are governed despite the fact that enacting education policy is considered a role of state government. In contrast, the Bill of Rights do not apply the same way to private schools because they are not a governmental entity.

A variety of sources of federal and state law exist. Primary sources of law have been defined as "the law itself" (Russo, 2006, p. 8). Primary sources include a variety of types of federal and state law such as "constitutions, statutes (and their legislative histories), regulations (along with administrative decisions and rulings that interpret them), and case law" (Russo, 2006, p. 8). Primary sources of law are created by all three branches of the U.S. government: the executive, legislative, and judicial branches. The executive branch authorizes agencies such as the U.S. Department of Education to draft regulations. Congress, which comprises the federal legislative branch, enacts federal laws. Courts such as the state supreme courts interpret the law to create binding precedents.

The supreme source of primary law is found in federal and state constitutions. As the primary law of the United States, the U.S. Constitution provides the framework for the American legal system. State and federal governments must follow the U.S. Constitution, but state constitutions and statutes are supreme in their state jurisdictions as long as they "do not contradict or limit rights protected under their federal counterpart" (Russo, 2006, p. 8). Thus, the judiciary (or court system) often reviews statutes, regulations, state constitutions, and case law to determine whether it aligns with the U.S. Constitution.

Because public school employees and students have rights guaranteed by the U.S. Constitution, it is vital to understand the three most important constitutional amendments that impact school law: the First (dealing with free speech and religion), the Fourth (concerning search and seizure) and the Fourteenth Amendment (concerning due process and equal protection). They are found within the Bill of Rights, which is comprised of the first 10 amendments to the U.S. Constitution and "safeguards individual liberties against governmental encroachment" (Russo, 2006, p. 9). The most applicable amendment to legal issues involving students with disabilities is the Fourteenth Amendment, Section 1. (There are 5 sections, but Section 1 is relevant to education law): No state shall make or enforce any law which shall abridge the privileges or immunities of citizens of the United States; nor shall any state deprive any person of life, liberty, or property, without due process of law [Due Process Clause], nor deny to any person within its jurisdiction the equal protection of the laws [Equal Protection Clause] (U.S. Constitution, amendment XIV, § 1).

Another example of a primary source of law is a statute that is passed by a legislative body such as a state legislature (state statute) or Congress (federal statute). Statutes are also referred to as *laws* or *legislation*. Statutes that are grouped together by subject matter are called *codes*. After statutes have been enacted, they have authority until they have been amended or rescinded by the legislature or deemed unconstitutional by a relevant court (Romantz & Vinson, 2009). Courts "interpret the meaning and application" of statutes, but they cannot change the language of laws (Romantz & Vinson, 2009, p. 5). Although the legislature may enact a general legal rule, it is often then interpreted and applied to specific cases by the judiciary, or courts.

Educational leaders must understand what the language of the statute means and how it should be applied. To do this, you should look to regulations and court cases that relate to the statute. The applicability of a given court opinion is based on the similarity of the facts of the case for which the opinion was rendered to the controversy that is being examined and on the authority of the deciding court.

Examples of federal statutes that are important in special education law include:

- *Individuals with Disabilities Education Act (IDEA)*. Prohibits discrimination against students with disabilities in schools receiving federal funding.

- *Section 504 of the Rehabilitation Act of 1973 (Section 504).* Prohibits discrimination against individuals with disabilities in programs receiving federal financial assistance.
- *Americans with Disabilities Act (ADA).* Prohibits discrimination against individuals with disabilities, and ensures equal opportunity for persons with disabilities in employment, state and local government services, public accommodations, commercial facilities, and transportation (applies to private and public entities).

Whereas statutes are the actual law, regulations are supplements to the law. They indicate how the law should be interpreted and implemented. Administrative agencies such as the Indiana Department of Education or the U.S. Department of Education draft regulations. Collectively, the regulations made by administrative agencies are referred to as *administrative law.* To illustrate, in Indiana, regulations are part of the Indiana Administrative Code (IAC). You can see what the IAC looks like by accessing http://www.in.gov/legislative/iac/. A well-known Indiana education regulation is Article 7, which outlines special education procedures that Indiana public schools must follow. It is part of Title 511 of the IAC, which is titled "Indiana State Board of Education." You can see what it looks like by accessing http://www.in.gov/legislative/iac/T05110/A00070.PDF.

One of the most important sources of law is case law. Case law, which is also sometimes referred to as *common law,* describes the collective body of law that is derived from the court opinions (Romantz & Vinson, 2009). Some have made the distinction that common or case law is law that judges make, whereas statutes are the law enacted by legislatures such as Congress and state representatives. Although the traditional role of the judiciary is to interpret the application of the law by making decisions when parties disagree about how the law should be interpreted, courts actually create binding law as a result of their decisions. For example, courts make law by deciding cases (lawsuits between parties) by interpreting legal principles (Romantz & Vinson, 2009). Because each case has a unique set of facts, new binding precedent is created every time a case is decided. The judiciary also makes law by interpreting the existing law such as constitutions, statutes, and regulations (Romantz & Vinson, 2009).

Courts must abide by certain doctrine such as precedent and *stare decisis.* A precedent is a past court decision. The legal principle requiring courts to use precedent when deciding similar cases is known as *stare decisis.* When considering emerging questions, you must analyze past decisions that have considered the same issue (Russo, 2006, p. 7). *Stare decisis* provides continuity in court decisions so that you can predict how future courts may decide a case. For example, in the future, perhaps you will want to persuade an audience to support a position you have. If there are past cases that support your position, then you can use them to argue that your position should be followed. However, if the precedent runs counter to your position, then you could argue that the current situation differs from the past cases. When educators are challenged about their decisions, it is helpful for them to be able to point to past precedent to support why they acted the way they did.

When deciding new cases, courts research and rely upon precedent for guidance. The judiciary is primarily organized in a federal and a state hierarchical system. Federal courts only decide cases involving federal questions or constitutional issues, whereas the state courts decide cases involving any issues and disputes related to state and constitutional law. However, administrative agencies such as state departments of education are often given authority to resolve disputes related to their organization. These cases are heard in separate systems called *administrative courts*. The reasoning behind administrative courts is for those with the expertise in a particular area to handle the dispute if possible. So instead of judges who may not be well-versed in the intricacies of special education, there are administrative law judges (ALJs) with more specialized training to decide special education disputes. In summary, there are three different types of court systems: state, federal, and administrative.

The federal court system and most state court systems are comprised of three tiers. The lowest level of both federal and state courts is the trial court. The next tier is the intermediate appellate court. The third tier is the highest appellate court. Thus, in the federal court system, the highest court is the U.S. Supreme Court, followed by the U.S. Circuit Courts of Appeal, and then the U.S. District Courts. The highest level of the state court system is typically the state supreme court, followed by the state court of appeals, and then the trial courts, which are often referred to as district, superior, or circuit courts. Appellate courts review lower court decisions and actions after an appeal has been filed. Typically, appellate courts do not review the factual determinations of the lower courts, but instead only review alleged errors of law that appear in the lower court's record.

State and federal systems are independent, with the exception of the U.S. Supreme Court. Supreme Court opinions are binding for all other U.S. courts regardless of whether they are part of the federal or state system. The federal appellate courts are divided into 13 circuits. Every state and U.S. territory has at least one federal district court (Barkan, Mersky, & Dunn, 2009).

There are two main types of jurisdiction: subject matter and geographic jurisdiction. Although courts have to follow precedent, they do not have to follow *all* precedent. Instead, they only must follow the precedent within their jurisdiction. Therefore, subject matter jurisdiction limits the type of cases that a court can consider. For instance, a federal court is prohibited from deciding cases about state law if there are no additional federal questions involved in the case.

Geographic jurisdiction restricts a court from deciding cases outside of the physical boundaries assigned to that court. Moreover, a court's decisions and laws made by legislatures are binding only within their assigned geographical area (Barkan et al., 2009, p. xxxii). An example of a geographic boundary is that the U.S. 7th Circuit Court of Appeals has geographic jurisdiction over the federal courts in Indiana, Illinois, and Wisconsin; thus, a court in California, which is in the 9th Circuit Court of Appeals, would not be bound to a 7th Circuit Court ruling.

REFERENCES

Barkan, S. M., Mersky, R. M., & Dunn, D. J. (2009). *Fundamentals of legal research* (9th ed.). New York, NY: Thomas Reuters/Foundation Press.

Individuals with Disabilities Education Act, 20 U.S.C. §§ 1400 et seq., 34 C.F.R. §§ 200 et seq

McCarthy, M. M., Cambron-McCabe, N. H., & Eckes, S. E. (2014). *Public school law: Teachers' and students' rights* (7th ed.). Upper Saddle River, NJ: Pearson.

Romantz, D. S., & Vinson, K. E. (2009). *Legal analysis: The fundamental skill* (2nd ed.). Durham, NC: Carolina Academic Press.

Russo, C. (2006). School law and research in the 21st century. In S. Peruth & R. Mawdsley (Eds.), *Research methods for studying legal issues in education.* Dayton, OH: Education Law Association.

U.S. Constitution, amendment XIV, § 1.

Index

Activities
  Dating Game with a Twist, 58, 64–67
  Disability Law Scenario Activity, 20, 22–27
  discipline of students with disabilities, 71, 74–78
  eligibility for special education services, 36–39
  federal entitlements and protections, 22–27
  Historical Background/Current Events Game, 8.11–14
  Individualized Education Programs (IEPs), 47–52, 96–97
  "You Make the Call" Game Show, 36–39
A.C. v. Shelby Cnty. Bd. of Educ. (2013), 19
ADA. *See* Americans with Disabilities Act (ADA) of 1990
Administrative courts, 104
Administrative law, 103–104
Administrative law judges (ALJs), 104
Adult independent living skills, 86, 89–90
Adverse effect requirement, 34–35, 40
African American students, identification as needing special education, 13, 15
A.G. Bell Association, 95
Algozzine, B., 7
Allergies, 13–14, 28
Alternative dispute resolution (ADR), 94, 95, 97–99
Americans with Disabilities Act (ADA) of 1990, 8, 9, 19–22
  comparison of laws, 24–25, 27–31, 37
  definition of disability, 34–35
  described, 103
  Disability Law Scenario Activity, 20, 23–24
  discrimination against individuals, 23–25
  eligibility for special education services, 33–38
  federal entitlements and protections, 23–25
  key features, 23–25
  parent/guardian lawsuits under, 28
  physical impairment, defined, 34–35
Amren, K., 94
Appellate courts, 104
Applied Behavior Analysis (ABA), 25, 26
Ashland Sch. Dist. v. Parents of R.J (2009), 56
Assistive technology evaluations, 45
Attention Deficit Disorder (ADD), Individualized Education Programs (IEPs), 47–52
Attention Deficit Hyperactivity Disorder (ADHD), 24
  discipline of students with disabilities, 71
  eligibility for special education services, 38–39
  Individualized Education Program (IEP), 55
  least restrictive environment (LRE), 60, 62, 63
Autism
  disability category, 34
  discipline of students with disabilities, 70, 71, 72, 79
  eligibility for special education services, 38–39
  family-school relationships, 95–96
  Individualized Education Programs (IEPs), 44, 45
  least restrictive environment (LRE), 60, 62, 63–64
  Section 504 entitlements, 25, 26

Barkan, S. M., 104
Bartlett, L. D., 96
Bd. of Educ. of Hendrick Hudson Sch. Dist. (1982), 43
Behavioral Intervention Plans (BIPs), 70, 71, 72, 77–79
Benz, M. R., 15
Berlin, L. F., 1–2
Beyond High School Brainstorming Exercise, 85–86
Bill of Rights, 102
Bisbee Unified Sch. Dist. (2010), 70, 80
Blake, J. J., 15
Blindness, 34
Board of Education v. Rowley (1982), 12, 46
Brown v. Board of Education, 12
Bullying in schools, 14, 15
Butler, J., 70

Cambron-McCabe, N. H., 101
Case law, 103
Child Find, 22–23, 27
Chronic fatigue syndrome, eligibility for special education services, 38, 39
Clubfeet, 26, 27, 34
Cochlear implants, 25, 26–27, 38, 39
Codes, 102
Cole, H., 8
Common law, 103
Connecticut Department of Education, 14
Constitutional amendments, 102
Constitutional law, 101–102
Continuum of placements, 61, 64–67
Controlled Substances Act of 1970, 80
Cope-Kasten, C., 15
Court system, 104
CTL v. Ashland Sch. Dist. (2014), 13–14

Daniel R.R. v. State Bd. of Educ. (1989), 68
Dating Game with a Twist, 58, 64–67
Davidson, D. N., 7
Deaf-blindness, 34
Deafness, 34
Death of students, 7, 14, 71
Definition Cards, discipline of students with disabilities, 71, 74–78
Deliberate indifference, 14
Developmental delays, 34
  Individualized Education Programs (IEPs), 53–54
  least restrictive environment (LRE), 65, 66
Diabetes, 13–14, 19, 24, 28
Disability Law Scenario Activity, 20, 22–27
Disability Rights Education & Defense Fund, 37
Discipline of students with disabilities, 70–83
  activity, 71, 74–78
  additional resources, 82–83
  background, purpose, and objectives of the lesson, 73–74
  Definition Cards, 71, 74–78
  Discipline Scenarios, 71–73, 79–81
  emergency exceptions for immediate removal, 75–76
  expulsion, 72, 73–74, 79
  facilitator script, 73–74
  hook, 71–73
  under IDEA *versus* Section 504, 80–81
  Individualized Education Programs (IEPs), 70, 72, 79, 80–81
  Interim Alternative Educational Settings (IAES), 71, 77–78, 80
  introduction for facilitators, 70–71
  Legal Violations Skit, 71, 81–82
  Manifestation Determination, 70–73, 75, 76, 78, 79, 81
  materials needed, 71
  questions for conversation, 78–81
  restraints, 7, 14, 71
  seclusion, 7, 14, 71
  suspension, 7, 72–76, 79
  10-day rule, 76, 81
  test your knowledge, 81–82
  unidentified students with disabilities, 78
Discipline Scenarios, 71–73, 79–81
Discrimination against individuals, 9–10, 13–15, 23–25
Doug C. v. State of Hawaii Dept. of Ed. (2013), 19, 95
Drug Enforcement Agency, 80
Drugs/controlled substances, discipline of students with disabilities, 75, 80
Due process protections, 12, 15, 74, 98, 102
Duffett, A., 84
Dunn, D. J., 104
Dyslexia, least restrictive environment (LRE), 60, 62

Eberwein, H. J., 2
Eckes, S. E., 1, 101
Educational Benefit Game, 44, 53–56
Education for All Handicapped Children Act (P.L. 94-142) of 1975, 9, 12, 19, 21
Eligibility for special education services, 33–42
  activity, 36–39
  additional resources, 41
  background, purpose, and objectives of the lesson, 36
  extent of, 10
  facilitator script, 36
  growth of, 10
  hook, 35
  introduction for facilitators, 33–35
  local educational agency (LEA) evaluation, 23, 27
  materials needed, 35
  questions for conversation, 40
  Student Special Education Eligibility Scenarios, 38–39
  test your knowledge, 40–41
  Who Is Eligible Chart, 35, 37
  "You Make the Call" Game Show, 36–39
Emergency exceptions for immediate removal, 75–76
Emotional disturbance
  disability category, 34
  discipline of students with disabilities, 72, 79
  Individualized Education Programs (IEPs), 54, 55
  least restrictive environment (LRE), 60, 62, 66
Employment and career training, 86, 89, 90
Etscheidt, S., 96
Expulsion, 12, 72, 73–74, 79

Facilitator scripts
  discipline of students with disabilities, 73–74
  eligibility for special education services, 36
  family-school relationships, 96
  federal entitlements and protections, 21–22
  Individualized Education Programs (IEPs), 44–45
  learning about special education law, 9–11
  transition services, 87
Family-school relationships, 94–100. *See also* Parents/guardians
  activity, 96–97
  additional resources, 100
  alternative dispute resolution (ADR), 94, 95, 97–99
  background, purpose, and objectives of the lesson, 96
  case scenario, 95–96
  facilitator script, 96
  hook, 95–96
  introduction for facilitators, 94
  materials needed, 94–95
  Procedural Safeguards: Parents' Right to Participate in the IEP Process of Their Child, 95, 99
  questions for conversation, 97–99
  test your knowledge, 99–100
  Top Ten Methods to Foster IEP Team Collaboration, 95, 97
Fantz, A., 70
Farmer, J., 84

Federal entitlements and protections, 19–32
activity, 22–27
additional resources, 31–32
background, purpose, and objectives of the lesson, 21–22
comparison of laws, 23–25, 27–31, 37, 80–81
Disability Law Scenario Activity, 20, 22–27
facilitator script, 21–22
Fill-In-The-Blank Worksheet, 20, 29–31
hook, 20–21
introduction for facilitators, 19–20
materials needed, 20
questions for conversation, 27–28
test your knowledge, 28–31
Fill-In-The-Blank Worksheet, 20, 29–31
First Amendment, 102
Fisher v. Bd. of Educ. of Christina Sch. Dist., 62
Fostering IEP Team Collaboration exercise, 96–97
Fourteenth Amendment, 102
Fourth Amendment, 102
Free Appropriate Public Education (FAPE)
defined, 23
disability-based harassment, 14
discipline of students with disabilities, 70, 77–78
legal challenges, 43, 44
Section 504 entitlement, 25, 26
student eligibility for special education services, 33
two-part test, 12
Functional Behavioral Assessments (FBAs), 71–74, 77

Games
Dating Game with a Twist, 58, 64–67
Educational Benefit Game, 44, 53–56
Historical Background/Current Events Game, 8, 11–14
"You Make the Call" Game Show, 36–39
Garda, R. A., 15, 33
G.J. v. Tuxedo Union Free Sch. Dist. (2004), 64
General education classrooms
impact of placement of students with disabilities, 68
Individualized Education Programs (IEPs), 52
special education classrooms *versus*, 10, 12, 53–54, 65, 66
special education students in, 1, 23
Geographic jurisdiction, 104–105
Goldberg, Doug, 97

Hartmann v. Loudoun Cnty. Bd. of Educ. (1997), 68
Hearing impairment
disability category, 34
discipline of students with disabilities, 72, 79
eligibility for special education services, 38, 39
Individualized Education Programs (IEPs), 54, 55
least restrictive environment (LRE), 66
parent/guardian lawsuits concerning, 28
Section 504 entitlements, 25, 26–27
Henderson, A. T., 94
Herbst, M., 1, 7, 10

Highly qualified teachers, 13
Historical Background/Current Events Game, 8, 11–14
HIV/AIDS, 28
Home placement, discipline of students with disabilities, 73, 79
Honig v. Doe (1988), 33, 74
Hook (anticipatory set)
defined, 4–5
discipline of students with disabilities, 71–73
eligibility for special education services, 35
family-school relationships, 95–96
federal entitlements and protections, 20–21
Individualized Education Programs (IEPs), 45–46
instruction in special education law, 9
least restrictive environment (LRE), 59
Hook, transition services, 85–86
Hospitalization, special schools *versus*, 54, 55, 66, 67

IDEA Amendments of 1997, 12–13
IEP Annual Review Role-Play, 47–52
IEPs. *See* Individualized Education Programs (IEPs)
Inclusion, 23
Indiana Department of Education, 103
Individualized Education Programs (IEPs), 43–57
activity, 47–52
additional resources, 56
attendance at IEP meetings, 52–53
background, purpose, and objectives of the lesson, 44–45
defined, 8, 12
discipline of students with disabilities, 70, 72, 79, 80–81
eligibility for special education services, 36
facilitator script, 44–45
family-school relationships, 96
hook, 45–46
IEP Annual Review Role-Play, 47–52
introduction for facilitators, 43–44
Manifestation Determination, 70–73
materials needed, 44
questions for conversation, 52–53
sample classroom observation notes, 50–51
sample IEP program, 49
sample IEP program meeting agenda, 48
sample IEP program meeting notice, 48
sample IEP program meeting script, 45–46
sample present levels of educational performance, 49–50
test your knowledge, 53–56
transition services, 53. *See also* Transition services
violation of requirements, 19
Individuals with Disabilities Education Act (IDEA) of 1990, 9, 12, 19–23, 25–28, 95–96, 98
Amendments of 1997, 12–13
comparison of laws, 24–25, 27–31, 37, 80–81
definition of disability, 33–34, 40
described, 102
disability categories, 33–34

Individuals with Disabilities Education Act (IDEA), *continued*
Disability Law Scenario Activity, 20, 22–23
discipline of students with disabilities, 70, 76–77, 80–81
eligibility for special education services, 33–40
extent of use and eligibility for services, 10
federal entitlements and protections, 22–23
funding issues, 15, 101
Individualized Education Programs (IEPs). *See* Individualized Education Programs (IEPs)
key features, 22–23
least restrictive environment (LRE) requirement, 58, 59. *See also* Least restrictive environment (LRE)
Manifestation Determination, 70–73, 75, 76, 78, 79, 81
purpose behind, 16
reauthorization of 2004, 8, 12, 15, 84–85, 87–88, 99
significance for educators, 19
"Stay Put" provision, 67
Individuals with Disabilities Education Improvement Act (2004), 12–13
Institute of Education Sciences, 1, 7
Institutionalization, special schools *versus*, 54, 55, 66, 67
Integration of students with disabilities, 12
Intellectual disabilities, 12, 13
disability category, 34
Individualized Education Program (IEP), 56
mental impairment, defined, 35
Interim Alternative Educational Settings (IAES), 71, 77–78, 80
Iowa City Community School District, 13

Jackson v. Northwest Local Sch. Dist. (2010), 70, 78, 79
Jennifer D. v. New York City Dept. of Educ. (2008), 63–64
J.H. v. Fort Bend Indep. Sch. Dist. (2010), 54, 65, 66
Johnson, J., 84
Johnson, S. F., 84
J.P.M. v. Palm Beach County Sch. Bd., 71
Jurisdiction, 104–105

Katsiyannis, A., 1, 7, 10, 70, 73–74, 84
K.C. v. Mansfield Indep. Sch. Dist.(2009), 56
Keeping All Students Safe Act (KASA) of 2013, 14, 70
King v. Pioneer Reg'l Educ. Serv. Agency, 71
K.I. v. Montgomery Pub. Sch. (2011), 45
K.M. v. Tustin Unified Sch. Dist. (2013), 28

Lake, S. E., 61, 63
Learning about special education law, 1–2, 7–18
activity, 11–14
additional resources, 16
background, purpose, and objectives of the lesson, 9–11
facilitator script, 9–11
Historical Background/Current Events Game, 8, 11–14
hook, 9
introduction for facilitators, 7–8
materials needed, 8
questions for conversation, 15–16
test your knowledge, 16
Learning disabilities (LD), 13
disability category, 34
discipline of students with disabilities, 73, 79
least restrictive environment (LRE), 60, 62
Least restrictive environment (LRE), 12, 58–69
activity, 64–67
additional resources, 69
background, purpose, and objectives of the lesson, 59–64
continuum of placements, 61, 64–67
Dating Game with a Twist, 58, 64–67
hook, 59
introduction for facilitators, 58
LRE Concept Map, 58, 68, 69
LRE Law Scenarios Worksheet, 58, 59, 60–64
materials needed, 58
nature of, 58
questions for conversation, 67–68
Section 504 entitlement, 25, 26
test your knowledge, 69
year-to-year changes, 68
Legal Violations Skit, 71, 81–82
Local educational agencies (LEAs)
evaluations to determine eligibility, 23, 27
funding issues, 15, 28, 101
LRE Law Scenarios Worksheet, 58, 59, 60–64
procedural protections, 23, 27
Logsdon, A., 43
Long v. Murray County Sch. Dist. (2013), 14
Losinski, M., 1, 70, 73–74
LRE. *See* Least restrictive environment (LRE)
LRE Concept Map, 58, 68, 69
LRE Law Scenarios Worksheet, 58, 59, 60–64
Lund, E. M., 15

Madeline P. v. Anchorage Sch. Dist, 63
Mainstreaming, 23
Manchin, A. C., 44
Manifestation Determination, 70–73, 75, 76, 78, 79, 81
Mapp, K. L., 94
McCarthy, M. M., 101
Mediation, 98
Medical conditions
allergies, 13–14, 28
assistive technology evaluations, 45
diabetes, 13–14, 19, 24, 28
parent/guardian lawsuits concerning, 28
Mental impairment, defined, 35
Mersky, R. M., 104
Metro. Bd. of Pub. Educ. v. Bellamy (2004), 70
M.H. v. Monroe-Wodbury Cent. Sch. Dist. (2008), 55, 65, 67
Militello, M., 1, 2

Mills v. Board of Education (1972), 12
Mueller, T. G., 94
Multiple disabilities
  disability category, 34
  Individualized Education Programs (IEPs), 44–45
Muscular difficulties, 71

National Dissemination Center for Children with Disabilities (NICHCY), 99
National School Boards Association (NSBA), 13–15
National Secondary Transition Technical Assistance Center (NSTTAC), 85, 91–92
Nendel, E., 9
New Fairfield BOE v. Cortese (2005), 62
New Jersey Department of Education, 13
New Milford Bd. of Educ. v. C.R. (2011), 44
New Paltz Central School District v. St. Pierre (2004), 33, 41
No Child Left Behind (NCLB) Act of 2001, 13
Nowell, B. L., 94

Orthopedic impairment, 26, 27, 34
Other health impairment
  disability category, 34
  Individualized Education Program (IEP), 55–56

Parents/guardians. *See also* Family-school relationships
  disagreement about discipline of students, 79
  disagreement about placement, 67
  Individualized Education Programs (IEPs), 43, 45–53
  lawsuits concerning IEPs, 44
  lawsuits under Section 504 or ADA, 28
  procedural rights to involvement, 19, 23–26, 94, 95, 99
  student eligibility for special education services, 33, 40
Part B Regulations of 2006, 98
Pazey, B. L., 8, 9, 73
Pennsylvania Association for Retarded Citizens (PARC) v. Pennsylvania (1972), 12
Physical impairment
  defined, 34–35
  muscular difficulties, 71
  orthopedic, 26, 27, 34
  traumatic brain injury, 34, 72, 79
Porter v. Illinois State Bd. of Educ. (2014), 62
Positive Behavioral Interventions and Supports (PBIS), 71, 77
Post-secondary support. *See* Transition services
Precedent, 104
Preservice training. *See* Learning about special education law
Price, A., 84
Primary sources of law, 101–102
Prince, A. M. T., 1, 70, 73–74
Principals
  Individualized Education Programs (IEPs), 52
  need for instruction in special education law, 1–2, 7–18, 19–20
  prepackaged curriculum for special education law, 2–5
Private placement
  least restrictive environment (LRE), 67
  special education classrooms *versus*, 54, 55, 66
Procedural Safeguards: Parents' Right to Participate in the IEP Process of Their Child, 95
Professional development. *See also* Learning about special education law
  need for instruction in special education law, 1–2, 7–18, 19–20

Reasonable accommodations, 24, 27
Rehabilitation Act of 1973. *See* Section 504 of the Rehabilitation Act of 1973
Restraints, 7, 14, 71
Richland Sch. Dist. v. Thomas P., 79
Roblyer, M. D., 43
Romantz, D. S., 102, 103
Roncker v. Walter (1983), 68
Rothstein, L., 84
Rowley legal tests, 12, 46
Russo, C., 101, 102, 103

Sacramento City Unified Sch. Dist. v. Rachel H. (1994), 68
Salem, D. A., 94
Scenarios
  disability law, 20, 22–27
  discipline of students with disabilities, 71–73, 79–81
  Educational Benefit Game, 44, 53–56
  eligibility for special education services, 38–39
  family-school relationships, 95–96
  IEP Annual Review Role-Play, 47–52
  Individualized Education Program (IEP), 44, 47–52, 53–56
  least restrictive environment (LRE), 58, 59, 60–64
  transition services, 87–88, 89
Schimmel, D., 1, 2
School psychologists. *See also* Learning about special education law
  Individualized Education Programs (IEPs), 46, 52
Seclusion, 7, 14, 71
Section 504 of the Rehabilitation Act of 1973, 8, 9, 19–22, 80–81
  comparison of laws, 23–25, 27–31, 37, 80–81
  definition of disability, 13–14, 34–35, 40
  described, 103
  Disability Law Scenario Activity, 20, 23–24
  discipline of students with disabilities, 74
  discrimination against individuals, 23–25
  eligibility for special education services, 33–38, 40
  federal entitlements and protections, 23–25
  Free Appropriate Public Education (FAPE), 25, 26. *See also* Free appropriate public education (FAPE)
  key features, 23–25
  parent/guardian lawsuits under, 28
  physical impairment, defined, 34–35

Section 504 Plans, 24, 36, 80–81
Segregation of students with disabilities, 13–14
Serious bodily injury of students, 7, 75, 79, 80
Shelby, L., 73
Shuran, M. B., 43
Special education classrooms
  general education classrooms *versus*, 10, 12, 53–54, 65, 66
  private placement *versus*, 54, 55, 66
  special schools *versus*, 66
Special education law curriculum, 2–5
  organization of lessons, 4–5
  overview of lessons, 3–4
Special education laws
  basis legal framework, 101–105
  complexity of, 7–8
  discrimination against individuals, 9–10, 13–15, 23–25
  due process protections, 12, 15, 74, 98, 102
  lack of information in schools, 1–2
  litigation involving, 1, 7, 13–14
  need for instruction in, 1–2, 7–18, 19–20
  prepackaged curriculum for, 2–5
  relationship among laws, 24–25, 27–31, 37, 80–81
  role of school leaders, 2–5
  unintentional violation of rights, 1, 8
Special education leaders. *See also* Learning about special education law
  Individualized Education Programs (IEPs), 45–52
  need for instruction in special education law, 1–2, 7–18
  prepackaged curriculum for special education law, 2–5
Special schools
  hospitalization/institutionalization *versus*, 54, 55, 66, 67
  least restrictive environment (LRE), 60, 62, 66
  special education classroom *versus*, 66
Speech or language impairment, 34
Stare decisis, 103–104
State educational agencies (SEAs)
  funding issues, 15, 28, 101
  procedural protections, 23, 27
  state legislature as primary authority, 101
  Zero Reject and Child Find, 22–23, 27
Statute law, 102–103
"Stay Put" provision, of IDEA, 67
Student discipline. *See* Discipline of students with disabilities
Students of color, identification as needing special education, 13, 15
Student Special Education Eligibility Scenarios, 38–39
Students with disabilities. *See also specific types*
  bullying in schools, 14
  discrimination, 9–10, 13–15, 23–25
Subject matter jurisdiction, 104
Substantial activities, 35
Suicide, 14, 71
Suspension, 7, 72–76, 79

TASH, 70
Teachers. *See also* Learning about special education law
  highly qualified, 13
  Individualized Education Programs (IEPs), 45–52
  need for instruction in special education laws, 1–2, 7–18, 19–20
  prepackaged curriculum for special education law, 2–5
  special education *versus* general education, 10
Teaching Approach to Mastery (TAM), 60
10-day rule, 76, 81
T.F. v. Fox Chapel Area Sch. Dist. (2013), 13
Timothy W. v. Rochester (1989), 22–23
Top Ten Methods to Foster IEP Team Collaboration, 95, 97
Transition services, 84–93
  activity, 87–88, 89
  additional resources, 93
  background, purpose, and objectives of the lesson, 87
  Beyond High School Brainstorming Exercise, 85–86
  defined, 84–85
  described, 53
  facilitator script, 87
  hook, 85–86
  Individualized Education Programs (IEPs), 53
  introduction for facilitators, 84–85
  materials needed, 85
  National Secondary Transition Technical Assistance Center (NSTTAC) Indicator Checklist, 85, 91–92
  questions for conversation, 88–90
  Student Transition Services Under IDEA: Student Scenario, 87–88, 89
  test your knowledge, 90–92
  Transition Services and Post-High School Goals Activity, 85, 88
Traumatic brain injury
  disability category, 34
  discipline of students with disabilities, 72, 79

U.S. Circuit Courts of Appeal, 104–105
U.S. Constitution, 101–102
U.S. Department of Education, 9, 101, 103
  discipline of students, 70, 78, 80
  National Center for Education Statistics, 10
  Office for Civil Rights (OCR), 7, 19, 24
  Office of Special Education and Rehabilitative Services, 24
  Office of Special Education Programs, 98
U.S. District Courts, 104
United States General Accounting Office (GAO), 94
U.S. Government Accountability Office (GAO), 7, 14, 70–71
U.S. Office of Special Education Programs (OSEP), 24
U.S. Supreme Court, 33, 74, 104

Vinson, K. E., 102, 103

Visual impairment, 34

Weapons, discipline of students with disabilities, 72, 75, 79, 80
Weber, M. C., 24
Weisenstein, G. R., 96
Who Is Eligible Chart, 35, 37
Williams, J. L., 73
Williams syndrome, 56
Wilson Cnty. Sch. Sys. v. Clifton (2000), 55, 66
Woods v. Northport Pub. Sch. (2012), 44–45

Yates, J. R., 9, 73
Yell, M. L., 15, 19, 22, 33
"You Make the Call" Game Show, 36–39

Zero tolerance weapons policy, 72, 79
Zhou, Q. Z., 15
Zirkel, P. A., 44

About the Authors

Regina Umpstead (J.D., University of Michigan; Ph.D., Michigan State University) began her career as an assistant attorney general in Michigan. She then discovered her passion for education and, after earning her Ph.D. in education policy, joined the Educational Leadership faculty at Central Michigan University, where she is currently an associate professor. Dr. Umpstead's research interests explore the law and policy dimensions of special education, teacher ethics and evaluation, and charter schools. She has written numerous scholarly articles and the book *Professional Responsibility for Educators and the Michigan Code of Ethics* (2010).

Janet R. Decker (J.D., Indiana University; Ph.D., Indiana University) began her career as a special education teacher teaching students with autism. With a desire to affect policy change for students with disabilities, she received her law degree and Ph.D. in Education Policy Studies from Indiana University. Currently, Dr. Decker is an assistant professor at Indiana University's School of Education, where she teaches school law courses to undergraduate and graduate students. Her research focuses on legal issues related to special education, autism, and charter schools. Prior to joining IU's faculty, she was also a Fellow for IU's Maurer School of Law's Family and Children Mediation Clinic, a research associate at IU's Center for Evaluation and Education Policy, and an assistant professor at University of Cincinnati. In 2011, the Education Law Association awarded her the Joseph C. Beckham Dissertation of the Year Award.

Kevin P. Brady (Ph.D., University of Illinois) began his career as an assistant professor in the Department of Educational and Community Programs at The City University of New York (CUNY), Queens College, where he first developed his passion for preparing future school leaders for the varied and complex legal issues in today's schools. Currently, Dr. Brady is an associate professor in the Department of Curriculum and Instruction at the University of Arkansas in Fayetteville. One of his primary research and scholarly interests comprises legal issues involving students with disabilities. Dr. Brady is a former member of the Board of Directors of the Education Law Association and is on the editorial board of several journals, including *Education and Urban Society*, *Journal of Disability Policy Studies*, and *West's Education Law Reporter*. His peer-reviewed scholarship appears in a wide array of leading educational law, policy, and technology journals.

David Schimmel (J.D., Yale University) is professor emeritus at the University of Massachusetts Amherst, and is author or coauthor of over 75 articles and 7 books about law and education, including *Principals Teaching the Law: 10 Legal Lessons Your Teachers Must Know* (2010) and *Teachers and the Law,* 9th Edition (2015). He is the recipient of the Education Press Association of America's Distinguished Achievement Award for Excellence in Educational Journalism, the Education Law Association's McGhehey (lifetime achievement) Award, and the University of Massachusetts's Distinguished Academic Outreach Award. His current teaching, research, and writing focuses on promoting legal literacy for teachers.

Matthew Militello (Ph.D., Michigan State University) is the Wells Fargo Distinguished Professor in Educational Leadership at East Carolina University in Greenville, NC. He has held faculty positions at North Carolina State University (2008–2014) and the University of Massachusetts Amherst (2005–2008). Prior to his academic career, Militello was a middle and high public school teacher, assistant principal, and principal in Michigan (1992–2003). Militello has more than 50 publications, including 4 books: *Leading with Inquiry and Action: How Principals Improve Teaching and Learning* (2009), *Principals Teaching the Law: 10 Legal Lessons Your Teachers Must Know* (2010), *Principal 2.0: Technology and educational leadership* (2013), and *Reframing Community Partnerships for Education: Uniting the Power of Place and the Wisdom of People* (2015).